Nice
Teams
Finish
Last

Nice Teams Finish Last

The Secret to Unleashing
Your Team's Maximum Potential

Brian Cole Miller

⅄MACOM

American Management Association

New York • Atlanta • Brussels • Chicago • Mexico City • San Francisco
Shanghai • Tokyo • Toronto • Washington, D.C.

Bulk discounts available. For details visit:
www.amacombooks.org/go/specialsales
Or contact special sales:
Phone: 800-250-5308
Email: specialsls@amanet.org
View all the AMACOM titles at: www.amacombooks.org

This publication is designed to provide accurate and authoritative information in regard to the subject matter covered. It is sold with the understanding that the publisher is not engaged in rendering legal, accounting, or other professional service. If legal advice or other expert assistance is required, the services of a competent professional person should be sought.

Library of Congress Cataloging-in-Publication Data

Miller, Brian Cole
    Nice teams finish last : the secret to unleashing your team's maximum potential / Brian Cole Miller.
       p.   cm.
    Includes bibliographical references and index.
    ISBN-13: 978-0-8144-1393-7
    ISBN-10: 0-8144-1393-5
    1. Teams in the workplace.   2. Communication in organizations.   3. Interpersonal communication.   I. Title.

    HD66.M5438   2010
    658.4′022—dc22

                                                                            2009044569

About AMA
American Management Association (www.amanet.org) is a world leader in talent development, advancing the skills of individuals to drive business success. Our mission is to support the goals of individuals and organizations through a complete range of products and services, including classroom and virtual seminars, webcasts, webinars, podcasts, conferences, corporate and government solutions, business books and research. AMA's approach to improving performance combines experiential learning—learning through doing—with opportunities for ongoing professional growth at every step of one's career journey.

Printing number

10   9   8   7   6   5   4   3   2   1

Contents

Acknowledgments vii

Introduction ix

1. NICE Teams Are . . . Well, NICE! 1

2. The Opposite of NICE Is MEAN, Isn't It? 33

3. The Sweet Spot Between NICE and FIERCE: BOLD 59

4. BOLD Principles 85

5. BOLD Feedback 109

6. BOLD Requests 127

7. BOLD Disagreements 143

8. Become BOLD 161

Appendix 1: NICE Team Assessment 177

Appendix 2: Team Member Style Assessment 183

Appendix 3: BOLD Conversation Assessment 193

Appendix 4: BOLD Feedback Planning Sheet 197

Appendix 5: BOLD Request Planning Sheet 201

Index 205

About the Author 209

Acknowledgments

This book came from years of study and work with teams around the country. Thank you especially to my friends at Anthem FEP, Communico, VISA, Planned Parenthood, Wright-Ryan Construction, and Nationwide Insurance. Your examples of NICE, FIERCE, and BOLD teamwork in action taught me much.

Thank you Shellie Steinbaker and Greg Hund. I admire how open you are to others. You approach conversations from such a beautiful place of curiosity.

Thank you Lisa Alexander, Grace Dennison, and Alejandro Rodriguez. I have learned so much from your examples of how to give BOLD feedback.

Thank you Scott Shaffer for being a sounding board for my ideas for this book.

Thank you Lynne Franklin for helping me to say what I wanted to say, in a way that others would understand.

Thank you Lynn Jackson, again, for reading my nearly final manuscript and helping me fix it so it could become my final version.

Thank you Christina Parisi at AMACOM, for your patience as well as your confidence in me.

Thank you Heidee, Benjamin, Logan, and Tim. You are the most important team in my life: my family. Thank you for helping me learn and practice the principles of BOLD teams with you every day.

Thank you most of all Tim, for the many sacrifices you made so that I could write this book. Thank you for your neverending love, support, and encouragement.

Introduction

A few years ago, I was driving in southern Maine with a friend, talking about teams. I was lamenting how so many teams never quite realize their full potential. The team members all know what needs to happen for them to be wildly successful, but each is waiting for someone else to do it. Individual accountability is what's lacking, was my thought. My friend taunted me, "Brian, remember: There's no *I* in *team.*" I shot back, "Yes, but there's a *me* in there somewhere!"

Teams are made of individuals. They are a group of *me*'s. But as long as everyone keeps believing there is no *I* in *team,* they can continue to abdicate to others—often the team leader—the responsibility for their team's success. It shouldn't be all on the team leader's shoulders to make the team work. Each member has responsibility.

Is Your Team Too NICE?

This book is for people who want to step up and accept responsibility for the success of their team. Over the years, I've learned that the foundation of any team's success is open and honest communication. Unfortunately, our society has taught us that acting this way can hurt people; so we "play nice" with each other. In this book, I dispel the myths of NICE teams and show you how any team can become BOLD, simply by following some basic principles of communication.

If you are a NICE team, you will learn communication skills that will transform how you interact with each other. Because the focus is on individual responsibility, you need to know what is *not* in this book.

- I won't be teaching team leaders how to lead a team (except by example, as a member of the team).
- I won't be showing you how to create or lead a culture change, beyond the shift that naturally occurs when you apply the skills contained here.
- Nor will I be telling you how to resolve conflict. (What I will do, though, is give you the tools you need to avoid unnecessary conflict in the first place.)

Chapter 1 is all about NICE teams. I expose the seven myths that are common for teams that are stuck in NICE. Then I describe the nine classic team members. Each of them has his or her own motivation to be NICE.

There is a lot of information about the team member types, and here's why. If you're going to initiate or lead a change in your team's dynamics, you need to understand these types in order to improve your chances of success. Understanding how different things motivate people is critical to appealing to their collective conscience. The Team Member Style Assessment in Appendix 2 helps you identify which team member style you have, as well as the other styles found in your team, so that you can address them effectively.

When NICE teams realize that NICEness is stymieing their potential, they often err by going to the other extreme: FIERCE. In Chapter 2, I describe the seven myths of FIERCE teams, as well as how the nine team members adjust in a FIERCE environment.

Your Goal Should Be a BOLD Team

BOLD is the delicate balance between NICE and FIERCE. In Chapter 3, I show how the myths of NICE and FIERCE become *truths* for BOLD teams. When the nine kinds of team members rise to BOLDness, each can make a unique and valuable contribution.

Becoming BOLD

These are all good concepts, but how do you put them to work? That's what Chapter 4 is about. Here you find the four basic principles of BOLD communication. It all starts with how team members interact with each other. These principles can be applied to just about any interaction in a team setting.

The next three chapters show how to apply the BOLD principles to the most common team interactions.

- Chapter 5 is about giving feedback: how to share your reactions with others.

▫ Chapter 6 deals with making requests: how to ask for what you want or need from others.

▫ Chapter 7 covers disagreeing: how to share differing opinions and viewpoints.

In each chapter, I divide the topic into easy-to-follow steps built on the four basic BOLD principles.

Finally, Chapter 8 is for team leaders. The aim of this book is primarily to guide and encourage team members to become BOLD, so I won't get into traditional team leader topics (such as how to be a team leader, how to hold people accountable, or how to manage change). I *will* give you some direction, tips, and exercises for leading your team toward BOLD. You'll find even more help in the appendixes, where I've included assessments and worksheets that can help you apply what you learn from the book.

True, there is no *I* in *team*. But there is a *me*. And it's time for all of the *me*'s on your team to stop waiting around for somebody else to create the ideal team. So let's start with the *me* who's holding this book right now.

◆ ◆ ◆

Be bold, be bold, and everywhere be bold.

HERBERT SPENCER

Nice Teams Finish Last

1

NICE Teams Are...
Well, NICE!

It's nice to be nice . . . to the nice.

Frank Burns, *M*A*S*H*

"If you can't say something NICE, don't say anything at all!" That's my mother talking. And my Sunday school teacher. And every other adult from my childhood. And *your* childhood. Growing up, we heard this saying over and over. We were taught to keep our mouths shut. Don't talk back. Don't question authority. Don't have a different opinion. Don't rock the boat. Don't cause trouble.

In the workplace, we learn similar lessons. Never give real feedback. Don't ask for what you really want from others. Avoid conflict. Sugarcoat bad news. Don't be disagreeable. Make people feel good by telling them what they want to hear. Praise them when they fail: Praise helps them feel better about their failure. All this is done in the name of being NICE.

Play NICE. Be NICE!

When you're NICE, people get along. No one fights. No one has hurt feelings. Everyone is happy. Everyone belongs. And in the end, you get to sit in a circle holding hands with the other NICE people and sing "Kumbaya."

So goes the logic of being NICE.

The problem is that *it's just not true.* It is especially not true for teams. Time and again I've seen eager, ambitious teams play too NICEly together and not reach their potential. They're productive, no doubt, but often only marginally. *I've never seen a NICE team consistently exceed expectations or blow the competition out of the water. That's because NICE gets in the way of radical innovation, phenomenal customer service, and incredible operating efficiency.*

Granted, at first blush, the NICE team looks like a high-functioning team that has truly arrived! But it hasn't.

Where Teams Stall

Every successful team passes through four stages of team development. Bruce Tuckman introduced the terms *forming, storming, norming, performing* to reflect these stages.

◻ In *forming*, team members focus on clarifying goals, membership, and leadership. They often work independently as they figure out how they fit in as individuals.

- After the team forms, conflict is bound to happen because members have different ideas about how to accomplish the work. If handled poorly or if allowed to get out of control, this *storming* stage can actually lower the motivation of team members and make them fail. Handle it well, and the team is ready to move on.

- On the other side of storming is *norming*, where members learn to work together by resolving differences and normalizing how they'll approach work together. They figure out how they will interact with each other and what to expect from one another.

- Finally, they are *performing*. The members learn to depend on each other and become highly productive. They get the job done efficiently and effectively, without inappropriate conflict getting in the way. They may cycle back through the four stages intermittently (especially when the team membership changes) but quickly make it back to *performing*.

Although most NICE teams claim to be *performing*, they are not. They're stuck at the doors of *storming*. Dig a little and you'll find individual commitment is not strong. Team members are less than excited about what they're doing together and whom they are doing it with. Camaraderie is high among some members but quite low among others, although they try hard not to let the disharmony show. They do not feel interdependent (a real litmus test for a true team environment), but more like a bunch of people doing similar work and trying to get along.

Timothy Biggs adds another step to the model. He places *norming* between *forming* and *storming*. Then he renames the stage after *storming*, calling it "re-norming." In his version of the *norming* stage, the team's performance is acceptable. But the leader and/or the team prevent it from progressing through the *storming* stage toward truly high performance. The responsibility for team performance stays with the leader (not the team), and the team never passes *storming*. So it never achieves its true potential as a high-performing unit. This is usually where NICE teams stall.

Unwilling to venture into *storming*, NICE teams appear to function well on the surface, but they never excel. They meet most or even all of their goals, but rarely *exceed* them. It often takes everything they have to just hit expectations. They spend a lot of energy trying to manage what others expect of them, and they try to keep expectations within reach. They never experience quantum leaps in performance. Marginal improvements are all they hope for because, deep down, even they recognize their limitations.

Any conflict that does arise is dealt with quickly and efficiently—but not necessarily effectively. The goal of conflict resolution for a NICE team is not true resolution: The goal is a quick return to a superficial calm. A return to NICE. So a NICE team may step into *storming* briefly, but it retreats quickly to safe and familiar territory.

Why Teams Go NICE

NICE teams mistakenly believe that playing NICE is what cooperation and teamwork are all about. They believe that getting along requires people to be NICE to each other—all the time. They collectively believe the seven most common myths about NICE teamwork:

Myth 1: *We only praise each other, and we do it often!*

We have nothing but positive, uplifting things to say to each other. We don't waste time and energy criticizing each other or finding fault. Constructive feedback and developmental feedback are negative, and we don't need that stuff pulling us down. We all know our strengths and weaknesses and don't need anyone else pointing them out for us. Everyone loves working with such a positive, supportive bunch of people!

The Sad Truth: We really share only part of the story with each other. Our praise is usually vague and insincere. It consists of hollow platitudes and can even come off as dismissive. Constructive or negative comments are saved for private conversations far from the earshot of the person we're discussing. As comedienne Kathy Griffin explains, "Of course I talk about people behind their backs. Uh, it's called *manners!*"

So we don't help each other improve. Our positive feedback is not specific enough to truly reinforce beneficial behaviors. If we *do* try to give constructive feedback, it's usually so whitewashed or vague it has no real meaning. When truly helpful constructive feedback is actually given, we—or even the giver—quickly jump to the receiver's aid. We rescue the receiver from the feedback by justifying, excusing, or otherwise minimizing the quality and potential impact of the feedback.

We justify backbiting by calling it "venting" or "seeking help from a trusted colleague on a relationship issue." Some of us just bottle up our thoughts and feelings, and we explode every once in a while. When this happens, everyone is devastated. The person who blew is usually ostracized—at least temporarily—for breaking the peace or hurting someone's feelings.

Myth 2: *We stay focused on the task and don't get sidetracked by talking about things that aren't directly related to the task that needs to get done!*

Positive and optimistic, we come to agreement quickly and efficiently. We don't let negative thinking get us down. We are quick to take action!

The Sad Truth: We really don't plan well. We take action before we really think things through. We neglect contingency planning, assuming our course of action will work every time. We get caught up in groupthink and discourage differing opinions. We celebrate those with similar thoughts, approaches, and styles, thereby maintaining an environment that is far from diverse or inclusive.

So we dismiss those who want to play devil's advocate. When someone wants to look at the risks, we roll our eyes, become impatient, groan out loud, and dismiss them as quickly as possible. Calling them names like "Naysayer" or "Negative Nelly" or "Party Pooper" shuts them down pretty quickly. If not, the person who's leading the discussion can get personally offended by the push back. Their offense causes the devil's advocate to back down quickly for the sake of harmony and goodwill.

Only a few of us who are particularly invested in a topic will participate. The rest remain silent—and their silence is taken as agreement, even commitment. Even if they disagree, they stay silent—because we assume *that* is what cooperation and teamwork are all about. It doesn't take long for team members to learn not to speak out against the vocal minority. Because dissent is frowned upon, the final output is usually just adequate. Sometimes, however, we do end up reworking something that didn't go quite right. Team members who step in to solve a problem we didn't anticipate or plan for are often hailed as heroes.

Myth 3: *Our clients love us because we always find a way to say "yes!"*

We're not here to say "no" to them. It may be tough, but we'll find a way to include everyone's request on our master work plan. We'll do anything to keep them happy!

The Sad Truth: We really say "yes" to everyone because we are afraid to say "no." We haven't done the real work to get everyone in the team on the same page with our mission, vision, and strategy. As a result, we can't expect them to weigh an incoming request against our purpose and plans and make an intelligent decision. Without clarity and agreement on where we're going, we're unable to prioritize effectively. When we can't prioritize, we have no basis for saying "no" to anyone.

This strokes our egos to feel so wanted and needed!

So we miss targets and deadlines. We have good reasons (we're overwhelmed), but that doesn't help our reputation with key clients. We overload ourselves with work, and then we either have to work a lot of overtime or outsource some of the work to get it all done. We feel overworked (and underappreciated) a lot. We end up renegotiating deadlines and other commitments. Things may fall off the table—not deliberately and with purpose, but by oversight and from lack of planning and prioritization. And the more overwhelmed we feel, the more justified is our belief in Myth 2.

Myth 4: *We respect each other and the strengths each team member brings to the team!*

As acknowledged professionals, we don't doubt, challenge, or second-guess each other. Our leader is especially revered and respected. When our team leader makes a decision, we are saved the time and trouble of working out which way to go.

The Sad Truth: We really defer tough team decisions to our leader or to someone equally "deserving." Deference allows us to avoid having to wrestle with each other. We each put in our opinions without debate, and then look to our leader to choose. Or we defer team decision making to a team member who is deserving. A pecking order influences decision making. Team members who are closest to an issue or the most vested have more say than the rest of us. Those new to the team and those with lower positions in the organization have less say, regardless of their expertise or qualifications.

So *we* can't be held accountable if an *individual* makes the decision. And if that individual is the team leader, all the better because then we're sure of his or her support. If things don't go well, we're not to blame; so we're off the hook. Whatever the outcome, whoever was in agreement with the team leader will be perceived as having heightened influence with him or her—maybe even favored status. There are winners and losers. This status creates tension that goes unresolved until the next contest (read "team decision"). If someone other than the team leader decides, such as the person closest to the issue, we only have to support it half-heartedly. When the project fails, we can claim minimal involvement (and not look bad), while blaming the decision maker.

Myth 5: *We refrain from unnecessary conflict and confrontation!*

There's no place here for fighting and arguing. We get along well, and we all play NICEly together. Everyone likes each other and cooperates for the good of the team!

The Sad Truth: We really avoid all conflict and confrontation—even the necessary stuff. We sweep things under the rug so that we don't have to deal with the difficult stuff. We gloss over real problems. No one points out any elephants in the room. We don't deal with anything directly. We deal indirectly by pulling another person into our conflict, and we expect that person to negotiate some kind of resolution for us—without our having to do the work. We don't debate or even explore possibilities: We just talk around things. If a team member is brave enough to object to something, everyone else backs off the current position. The objection is not explored; it's accepted immediately and without question. Or it's countered with another statement that is then accepted immediately. Generally the last person to speak or the one who is most tenacious will get his or her way. We stay silent when we disagree, even if our point is valid or critical. We don't want to make waves. We deal with problems passive-aggressively.

So we never resolve real problems, and they keep coming back to haunt us. We end up creating all kinds of work-arounds: We work around issues or problems or even each other, instead of dealing with things. This tactic usually means more work, more time, or more expense. But we find it's worth it to avoid actually having to deal with the problem.

Myth 6: *We are open and flexible and freewheeling!*

We are always open to new information whenever it is available. We don't allow ourselves to be tied to agendas and timelines in meetings. We don't bind each other with roles and responsibilities, but remain flexible in how each of us approaches work.

The Sad Truth: We really only rarely make any real decisions. Each time we get close to a decision, we can get sidetracked easily by just about anyone or anything. Meetings drag on as we get caught up in tangents. When we *do* make a decision, it is always subject to revision when more information is available or when someone decides (later) to consider a new perspective. Questions must be answered on the spot—regardless of what we are discussing and how unrelated the question. If a question is asked, we must answer it right then (and go down that rat hole). We get easily distracted by issues that are easier or less dicey. It often feels like we're working in circles because we rarely come to resolution. Generally, the real decisions are made in private by a select few, including the leader and those closest to an issue.

So we remain unclear on our roles and don't confront each other to clarify them. We assume it's the team leader's job to do that. Decisions that do get made are supported only halfheartedly and are frequently reversed or altered later when new information is available. Reversing and altering decisions are done in private, with one or two members and the team leader. Communication following a meeting is rare. Shifting priorities make it almost impossible to hold anyone accountable for anything. Roles remain unclear, which allows team members to abdicate responsibility to others (with or without warning). People tend to approach work individually or independently so that they can't be blamed or associated with failure. ("Hey, at least *my* part went well!") The natural outgrowth is that people build their own turf. People build silos. People grab power and start taking credit individually. They don't have each other's backs. People build alliances behind the scenes.

Myth 7: *We are efficient!*

We don't waste time talking about feelings and emotions. We focus on the task, not on each other. When interpersonal relationship issues come up, we move to resolve them as quickly as possible so that they don't get in the way of the real work we're doing.

The Sad Truth: We really just brush over real interpersonal problems in the name of efficiency. When team members try to address interpersonal issues, the rest of us hush them with a desire to stay focused on the task at hand or to use our time most efficiently—on the work, not on relationships. All of a sudden, we violate our attachment to Myth 6, and the agenda becomes paramount. We have no time for so-called tangents, we must now stay within our time constraints. *We expect relationships to take care of themselves.* After all, how can there be any serious issues when everyone is so NICE to each other?

So resentment builds over unresolved issues. Playing NICE takes on a sinister tone. Individuals who feel wronged get passive-aggressive in their attempt to even the score because they are not permitted true resolution. Time and resources are wasted in attempts to sabotage the team's (or an individual's) effort for personal gain or revenge. Trust dissolves. Team members become suspicious of hidden agendas and ulterior motives. They work hard to protect themselves from each other.

How NICE is your team? Find out in Appendix 1.

Who Would Choose to Believe Such Myths?

Most NICE team players can be categorized as one of nine types (or perhaps some combination of them). They are willing, if not eager, to buy into the NICE team myths because they are one or more of nine personality types.

The Peacemaker: *Focused on team harmony and unity*

She can merge different ideas into one harmonious whole. In her quest for peace and harmony, she recognizes connections and interdependencies that may not be obvious to others. She readily sees the common thread that ties dissimilar and even conflicting opinions. She values the inputs of very different people and smoothly incorporates them into a unified position. She focuses on using similarities and differences to promote agreement and unity. She resents team members who confront others unnecessarily or angrily, disrupting the harmony she works so hard to maintain.

Her underlying questions are: "How can things run smoothly? How can we come together on this?"

Patient and nonjudgmental, warm and diplomatic, she makes her teammates feel understood, calmed, and accepted. But she struggles to take a position, vacillating endlessly between the pros and cons of both sides of an issue. With her passion for peace, she works hard not to make waves. She has become adept at seeing all sides of an issue so well that she can agree with anyone on any side of a discussion. In doing so, she is agreeable with everyone, even if agreement with one contradicts agreement with another. This vacillation makes for confusion among her teammates. They think she's *on* their side, when all she is doing is *seeing and appreciating* their side.

Here's the problem. Because she appreciates all sides of an issue, she tends to lose sight of her own position. She cannot contribute her own unique input. So teammates see her as indecisive or as someone who flip-flops on issues.

Desiring unity and harmony, she works to help others stay at peace by minimizing differences and smoothing them over. So real problems go unresolved and bad feelings fester, bound to surface later. When they do, they'll be stronger and more volatile—the very thing the Peacemaker wishes to avoid. While working so hard to keep the peace, the Peacemaker inadvertently comes across to her teammates as someone who avoids conflict, is slow to act, and maybe even weak. Her anger and frustration may come out passive-aggressively. To be more direct would mean disrupting the harmony she so desperately seeks. Unfortunately, her efforts to hang on to even an artificial peace are the very things that destroy it. Very real conflict is bound to come up with any team. And when it does, teammates go underground because the Peacemaker resists open resolution.

The Peacemaker believes that NICE keeps the peace, harmony, and unity. It doesn't.

The Champion: *Focused on power and influence*

He tends to approach work (and everything else in his life) with great gusto. He has a real passion for the work, and it comes out in his approach. He is intense—all about taking action. He may not always get his way, but everyone will always know he's been there! He will often be the first to speak up and suggest the team get moving.

"What action can we take *now*? How can we have greater impact here?"

Strong and confident, he makes his teammates feel empowered and well protected. He's got their back. Team members definitely feel as though they're part of the action around the Champion. But they can also feel steamrolled and inferior when he shows his full bravado.

The Champion places a great deal of value on being strong and honest. As such, he's more likely than others to speak out—bluntly. He is unaware of his impact on others, though. So when he thinks he's just "telling it like it is," others see him as being aggressive, domineering, or overbearing. NICE demands that he pull back on his tactless candor.

The Champion is a natural leader. When the team isn't making progress, he is likely to jump in, take the reins, and drive them forward. But in so doing, he can alienate others with his take-charge approach. The NICE team demands that he not ruffle feathers, even when ruffling feathers may be the very thing the team needs most!

On a NICE team, the naturally outspoken Champion holds back in order to avoid being ostracized. He learns quickly that when he stirs the pot by putting questions on the table, he is condemned. His teammates shun him and lose their respect for him. Rather than risk that alienation, he stays quiet. His strategy is to hold back to gain their respect. And the NICE team rewards him for his silent reserve and self-discipline. Unfortunately, in gaining that misplaced respect, he loses his passion for the work and checks out of the discussion more and more frequently.

The Champion believes that NICE allows him greater influence with the team. It doesn't.

The Perfectionist: *Concerned with the pursuit of excellence*

She is motivated by high personal standards and values. She constantly strives to improve things, including the tasks given to her. She strives to understand situations accurately and thoroughly before taking action. Her concern for detail means she keeps her teammates aware of very real limits, such as budgets or time constraints. She solves problems and finds the right decision by following proven methods and sound procedures. She prefers situations that require precision.

She asks, "What's the correct procedure? What's the right choice?"

Ethical and fair, self-disciplined and hardworking, she gives her teammates a sense of importance, competence, and high purpose. But inside she seethes with discontent at her own failings and shortcomings.

She sees the world in dualities: right and wrong, correct and incorrect, good and bad. Black or white is quite obvious to her, and she doesn't understand why others can't see how plain the difference is. Unfortunately, she has trouble seeing gray. All issues aren't quite so cut-and-dried as the Perfectionist wants to see them. She gets frustrated when her teammates don't see the "right" choice before them. They get frustrated when she sees only one "obvious" solution. With blinders on to various alternatives and options, she wants to press for the one and only correct answer, as she sees it. This singlemindedness leads her teammates to believe she is rigid or inflexible.

Given her high standards, she is critical of her teammates. But she doesn't speak up for fear of not being correct in her assessment or not delivering the feedback correctly. Unfortunately, her body language and attitude notify her teammates that she doesn't approve. As obvious as their shortcomings are to the Perfectionist, she is even more critical of her own. Relentless in her judgment and criticism of her own foibles, she is constantly giving herself critical feedback on just about everything.

The Perfectionist tends to be a hard worker—not necessarily a workaholic, but dedicated and committed to doing a good job and carrying her own weight. "Lazy" is rarely a word used to describe a Perfectionist. "Dependable," "reliable," "hardworking" are more like it. She expects everyone to be as dedicated and devoted as she is, and she quietly judges those who are not.

She also has a penchant for structure and order. She assumes that everyone appreciates having a proven process to follow, regardless of the task at hand. She offers or even forces a process on the team as a way of helping them all get it right. With structure, she is able to help her team stay on track and get the work done, despite their resentment.

The Perfectionist believes NICE means that they achieve excellence. It doesn't.

The Energizer: *Primarily concerned with innovation and enjoyment*

She believes life—and work—should be fun. She overflows with optimism and excitement for the team's efforts and success. She tends to see what *can be* rather than what *is*— possibilities and options more than actualities. She explores different ways to enjoy the team's work. She is curious about new ideas. She combines ideas into creative outcomes. She sees connections between seemingly unrelated topics in ways that are not evident to linear thinkers.

Her questions are, "What are the possibilities? How can we enjoy what we're doing?"

Fun-loving and spontaneous, confident and imaginative, she makes her teammates feel entertained, dazzled, and inspired. But she loses interest quickly when she's not having fun or being challenged enough.

A visionary, the Energizer can see great potential in all situations. Focused only on the bright side, though, she prefers planning to doing and tends to overpromise with her grand plans. But when it comes time to do the work— especially if it's less than exciting or involves attention to a lot of details—she pulls back (often to focus on something new and more interesting). Teammates feel she's doing all the driving and none of the doing. This gives her a reputation of being poor at follow-through. When things fail, she assumes her plans were flawless; so she blames her teammates—the implementers.

She is impatient with the status quo and also the lack of progress. Her desire for results leads to impulsive behavior.

This, combined with her optimistic approach, causes her to make plans that can be out of touch with the real world. When she is not taken seriously, she is hurt and avoids or blames teammates.

A quick thinker and even quicker learner, she processes information quickly and can get easily bored. She's a natural multitasker. She tries to protect herself and others from the unpleasantness that comes with negative things, such as boredom or conflict and direct confrontation. She falsely assumes that if all her teammates just did their jobs, everyone would have a good time and accomplish something truly great in the process. Engaging and optimistic, she can be very compelling. So she is frustrated by team members who can't see her vision for the future or who don't buy into it. Negativity is unwelcome.

She is reluctant to make decisions that cut off possibilities and options. For this, teammates view her as indecisive. Speaking up may ruffle feathers and cause unpleasantness among the team. The lack of dissension stifles the team.

The Energizer believes that NICE keeps the team fun and innovative. It doesn't.

The Guardian: *Focused on trust and security*

He is committed and loyal to his friends, family, and teammates. He is responsible and hardworking for the good of the team. Very tuned in to the relationships on the team, he is keenly aware of who is aligned with whom—on the team or outside it. Ever protective of his teammates, he is well connected to them. "Supportive," "compassionate," and "playful" are terms his teammates would use to describe him.

He asks, "Whom can we count on? What's going on beneath the surface?"

He stays on his guard and remains suspect of teammates' hidden agendas. Ambiguity increases his anxiety. He is slow to accept and trust others, especially leaders and other authority figures. Unsure of himself, he forgets or underplays his own power and capabilities. He tends to overestimate the power of others and ends up acquiescing to their pressure unnecessarily. He tests the rest of his teammates, and only after they've proven their trustworthiness does he accept them into his confidence.

Loyal and likeable, responsible and dependable, when he's engaged, he makes his teammates feel trusted, warm, and part of the team. His sense of humor is fun and welcoming. He's a hard worker and doesn't shirk responsibility. He comes alive when faced with adversity and can readily corral the troops to face difficulties with great success. The last one to "give up," he has real staying power when it comes to the team and its objectives.

A great listener, he is sometimes reluctant to speak his piece to those who are not considered confidants. When confronted by others he doesn't trust, he gets defensive and tends to deflect blame.

He is often plagued with doubt and uncertainty. Before making decisions or even taking a position, he explores potential hazards. To do so, he asks lots of questions and often plays the role of devil's advocate. Although he thinks he's helping the team understand the whole picture, he actually annoys them with his barrage of questions, suspicions, and second-guessing. The team interprets this as negativity, pessimism, or cynicism. Labeled a naysayer, he is often dismissed or shut down by a more optimistic team that doesn't want to deal with the "dark side." He fears they gloss over real threats. But speaking his mind may lead to being ostracized, so he holds back and worries in silence.

The Guardian believes NICE keeps the team together and safe. It doesn't.

The Observer: *Wants information to understand and be objective*

She tends to remain rational and detached. She craves information. She analyzes it and finds meaning in seemingly irrelevant data points. She looks for connections between ideas to fit them into a grander theory. She wants her theories to be backed by data. Her focus on strategy, information, and structure helps her team be systematic in its approach to making and implementing decisions.

Her questions are, "Are we being logical? What data supports our decision?"

Kind and open-minded, thoughtful and analytical, she makes her teammates feel welcome—as though they can make a contribution—and a little bit awed by her cool objectivity. But she doesn't like to deal with the social aspects of the team, making others feel bad for being human.

She prefers to conserve her energy and efforts. Believing that there's enough going on in the team, she sits back and observes others without jumping in. She watches and analyzes what's going on before she takes action—if she ever does. Sometimes she finds herself judging her teammates but is quiet about her conclusions on them. She is a sponge for information and knowledge but sometimes holds back on sharing everything. Teammates complain they don't know all the facts or can't tell where she stands on issues.

She needs to discover the meaning of facts and be certain of a solution before moving forward. Her reality is what is logical and measurable. Facts and figures are key for the Observer, who objectively deals with issues when the rest of the team gets tripped up on emotional attachments. As a result, she is slow to act and frustrates her teammates with her insistence on more data. They won't say anything, of course, but resentment can build on both sides as everyone continues to be NICE about their needs.

Objective and detached, the Observer is often seen as insensitive and uncaring. Her stand-back-and-observe style makes her less approachable or accessible than others. Patient, she assumes others will resolve any conflict quickly and dispassionately. She is less comfortable—sometimes even irritated—by the social niceties or pleasantries that others seem to need. She resents being forced to interact more than she chooses, and she doesn't appreciate team members' interrupting her privacy. Her teammates question whether she gets passionate about anything. When conflict arises, she withdraws rather than spending the energy required for resolution.

The Observer believes that NICE means plenty of information and objectivity. It doesn't.

The Individualist: *Longs for uniqueness and self-expression*

He is introspective and deep in his own thoughts and feelings. He is imaginative in his approach to tasks, creating unique results whenever possible. He sees possibilities in ordinary situations. He can put together seemingly unrelated things to make coherent wholes in unique and unusual ways. Everything he does, he does with flair and distinction.

He asks, "How do I feel about this? How can we express ourselves more creatively?"

Intuitive and open, he makes his teammates feel deep and special, understood and appreciated. But in his quest to fully understand himself, he can make others feel somewhat trivial or superficial if they don't share the same craving for deep self-examination.

The Individualist focuses on individuals in the team. He feels it's important for individuals to preserve their identities. He wants to create a team environment that respects team members' personal worth and dignity. Teammates should express themselves creatively and uniquely, but when he shares how he feels, the NICE team wants to hear only the positive or conforming. One-dimensional communication feels like censorship to the Individualist. Being authentic is critical to him; so, if he can't express himself fully, he'll not express much at all. Being denied his preference to full disclosure, he redirects his energy inward to deal with his feelings. Melancholy, maybe even depression, keeps him from spending much energy on the team.

Others need an outlet as well. So he engages them offline

to discuss their feelings about the work, their teammates, the team's direction, or anything else important to them. He enjoys being a confidant, helping teammates through a crisis, or making deep connections with them—albeit one on one, not in a team setting. Of course, these private discussions permit him to share himself as well.

The Individualist is intuitive and empathetic. And with his focus on others, he understands much of what's going on beneath the surface of a NICE team. But he holds his tongue. Speaking up would betray confidences he's garnered from others. Instead, he aids his team by helping them out individually. Because others don't have the full picture, he may be accused of manipulation. Nevertheless, helping (or overhelping?) makes him feel special in a team where conformity is expected and uniqueness is stifled.

The Individualist believes that NICE permits self-expression. It doesn't.

The Achiever: *Focused on productivity and results*

She has a penchant for action. She prefers action over getting or analyzing data, debating various viewpoints, or anything else that may delay productivity. Hardworking and competent, she carries more than her share of the team's load without complaint. Always busy, she is flexible when it comes to process as long as the team is making progress toward its goals. Quick and efficient, she often finds shortcuts to accelerate the pace.

Her questions are, "What's the objective? How will we get the results?"

Optimistic and confident, energetic and industrious, she makes her teammates feel empowered, part of the team, and capable of doing their best. But she doesn't have much patience for anything that (in her mind) slows the team down—things like emotion, conflict, or differences of opinion.

Driven to produce, she initiates action, easily taking control of conversations, meetings, and even the whole team to get things done. Compelled to win at all costs, she is highly competitive, even within the team. Success is measured in terms of meeting goals and objectives. She can come across as impatient and even domineering when faced with a deadline that she is committed to. Confronting others takes precious time away from being productive and doesn't directly contribute to the goal, so she avoids confrontation.

The Achiever needs to be perceived positively. Image-conscious, she works hard for the team to be successful. But if she sees the team is stuck, she breaks away from it, taking the work for which she's responsible. This way, *she* can still be successful. She overlooks the power that a team can have in making everyone look good—better than individuals can on their own.

Less concerned with exacting quality standards than with meeting commitments and deadlines, she is willing to cut corners to get ahead. In her hurry for results, she treats details lightly and is willing to sacrifice quality. She tends to *manage* problems instead of *solving* them. Her teammates see her willingness to put a spin on things as being dishonest, especially when she does it to them.

Achievers are often team leaders. In that role, they are

sometimes perceived as *using* the team to get results rather than *leading* it.

The Achiever believes that NICE will get the job done faster. It doesn't.

The Helper: *All about teammates and their needs*

He senses their needs and wants to help them out, sometimes to the point of overhelping. He connects well with others and helps everyone feel welcome and a part of the team. He appreciates the human element of the team and is constantly on the lookout for ways team members can depend on him for help and support.

He asks the questions, "How do others feel about this? What do my teammates need?"

Attentive and caring, warm and giving, he makes his teammates feel appreciated, fully heard, and taken care of. But he loses sight of the goals when he worries too much about helping his teammates.

Less concerned with facts and figures, he gets frustrated when team members get too task focused, forgetting the human element. He's more comfortable figuring out how team members relate to each other than determining how to accomplish a task. For him, appreciation has more personal meaning than does accomplishment. He can get so preoccupied with how his teammates are relating, he isn't clear on what he personally wants or needs.

The Helper is keenly aware of any hurt feelings, frustration, anger, resentment, or other underlying emotions on his team. He is disappointed when others aren't willing to help each other deal with the things that are getting in the way of a stronger, more supportive environment.

However, he is unwilling to risk hurting others by raising unpleasant issues. Instead, he overemphasizes the positive, hoping to help his teammates build confidence. He assumes that, with this confidence, they can then look inside and identify areas for improvement on their own. He doesn't want to be the one to point the finger, put someone on the spot, or cause hurt feelings.

A great socializer, the Helper likes interaction with his teammates. In his desire to help and support others, he often takes on more than he can handle and becomes inundated. Like the Guardian, he has trouble saying "no" to requests. He struggles to prioritize and falls further behind. Overwhelmed, he is frustrated with others who don't see his plight and offer assistance. It's even worse when he is not appreciated for all he does.

The Helper believes NICE means that everyone is happy together. It doesn't.

> Which of the team members are you most like? Find out in Appendix 2.

NICE Team Norms

Put all nine of these people on a team, and you get a set of NICE team norms. Newcomers are encouraged to conform to NICE.

Interestingly enough, on the surface, each NICE team player openly condemns NICE team behaviors. They all claim they want everyone to be open and direct and honest. But they refrain from doing so until everyone else does. No one wants to be the first to open up, the first to be honest, and the first to be direct. That's too risky!

NICE team players are not even aware that their own behaviors are the very things that keep them from getting what they really want. For example, the Peacemaker rarely sees that when she tries to minimize real differences, the conflict just goes underground and resentment builds. The team is not harmonious, despite the NICE facade. She doesn't realize that the *real* unity she desperately seeks is on the other side of the confrontation she works so hard to avoid.

The Achiever, in his efforts to keep everyone focused on the task, ignores the human element. What he misses is that, by addressing the people issues (especially early on), team members are then freed up to focus on the task, to fully commit to the goal. The very thing the Achiever seeks most—success—is more assured when everyone is working together toward that goal, rather than being dragged there by the ambitious Achiever.

Can these NICE team players be effective? Of course they can. They just don't reach their full potential. They become complacent with the NICE status quo. It's safer and more comfortable than what they see as the "obvious" alternative: a FIERCE team. So:

◻ The Peacemaker accepts pseudo harmony (with all the undercurrents) to avoid discord.

◻ The Champion lives with holding back (and denying the passion) to avoid losing influence.

- The Perfectionist goes along with being "good enough" (instead of true excellence) to avoid being wrong.

- The Energizer adapts to marginal innovation (that's far from exciting) to avoid unpleasantness.

- The Guardian lives with a fragile sense of security (that requires constant vigilance) to avoid standing alone.

- The Observer settles for simplicity (without being challenged) to avoid feeling overwhelmed.

- The Individualist ends up taking care of others (hoping others return the favor) to avoid feeling ordinary.

- The Achiever yields to busyness (rather than true success) to avoid failure.

- The Helper allows superficial relationships (without real feeling) to avoid giving offense.

Commitment among NICE team members is moderate at best. Their feelings of fulfillment are less than spectacular. They go about their business aware of the team's potential, but the realization of that potential seems just out of reach. They never imagine that being not so NICE may be part of the answer.

So if being NICE isn't the answer, what is—being mean? Not exactly. But understanding the other extreme (which I call FIERCE) helps explain the ideal: BOLD.

Summary

- Western culture teaches us to be NICE.
- NICE teams are stuck in the *forming* stage of team devel-

opment, unwilling to move through the *storming* stage, which leads them to heightened performance.

◻ There are seven myths about NICE teams, all of which promise false benefits and neglect the damaging consequences:

1. Give only positive feedback (thus giving only half the information).
2. Focus only on the task, and be ever optimistic (at the expense of good planning).
3. Never say "no" to clients (and miss deadlines by being overwhelmed).
4. Defer decision making to experts or to those in authority (and avoid team accountability).
5. Avoid conflict and confrontation (and allow problems to resurface over and over).
6. Remain open—never close the door on any decision (and avoid personal accountability).
7. Be efficient in all aspects (and let problems go underground).

◻ There are nine types of NICE team players, each with a different reason for promoting the NICE team environment:

1. The Peacemaker focuses on harmony (at any cost).
2. The Champion focuses on influence (and justice).
3. The Perfectionist focuses on excellence and quality (and what's right).

4. The Energizer focuses on enjoyment (and avoiding unpleasantness).

5. The Guardian focuses on security (and protecting self).

6. The Observer focuses on understanding (and remaining detached).

7. The Individualist focuses on uniqueness (and longing for what's missing).

8. The Achiever focuses on success (and avoiding people issues).

9. The Helper focuses on supporting others (and their feelings).

◻ The very things NICE team players seek are the things that elude them as they play too NICEly together.

◆ ◆ ◆

If you can't be kind, at least have the decency to be vague.

JUDITH MARTIN (MISS MANNERS)

2

The Opposite of NICE Is MEAN, Isn't It?

Give 'em Hell, Harry!

A HARRY S. TRUMAN SUPPORTER

So is the opposite of NICE mean? Not exactly. Rarely are team members downright mean to each other. In a team setting, the opposite of NICE is FIERCE.

At first glance, FIERCE teams may look like an appealing alternative to NICE. These teams are direct and to the point. Important feedback is shared. Individuals stand up for their needs. Ideas and opinions are challenged and debated. In fact, this is usually where NICE teams go when they want to become more effective.

Although they are seemingly the opposite on the surface, FIERCE teams and NICE teams are quite similar. Both have a singular (albeit opposite) focus that trumps the other. The NICE team's focus is on its members' needs and feelings. While NICE teams overemphasize their relationships, FIERCE teams pay little heed to them. A FIERCE team's singular focus is on the task, which requires absolute honesty if it is to be done well. Empathy for others takes a backseat to the task at hand. Action, success, and getting the job done trump any so-called people needs on the FIERCE team.

The FIERCE logic goes something like this:

- Let's be honest here—direct and to the point. There's the key to true success, and that's what it's all about: success!

- If we step on someone's toes along the way, so be it. We're all adults.

- It needed to be said, so let's be successful together and not worry about the little bumps along the way.

- We're fast-paced and always moving toward the target.

- We don't concern ourselves with the emotional baggage that bogs down those NICE teams.

With that logic, FIERCE teams can be successful too, just as NICE teams can. And just like NICE teams, they think they are in the *performing* stage of team development. They're not. They are stuck in *storming*. Little heed is given to relationships. Attention is fixed on the task, the goal, the results. Often the question, "May I be brutally honest?" precedes honesty that *is* brutal, a sure sign of *storming*, not *performing*.

NICE teams pursue success through—or at least with great respect for—relationships. FIERCE teams pursue success at the expense of them. FIERCE teams overemphasize the task or the goal, oblivious to relationships.

This focus on the task prevents team members from seeing the difference between a healthy debate and a truly harmful conflict. Just about anything goes on a FIERCE team, all in the name of getting the truth out and the job done. When conflict erupts, it's usually "every man for himself." Defensiveness runs high. Teammates forge alliances to survive, cope, or exert influence. Battle lines are drawn and redrawn. Each round reinforces these strategies, and FIERCE teams never emerge from the *storming* stage to enter the *norming* stage of team-building development.

In such a tumultuous setting, only the hardy thrive. Team commitment is low, and personal commitment high. Personal fulfillment, however, and camaraderie are low. There are constantly winners and losers. Turnover on the team is high.

Nevertheless, when NICE teams go FIERCE, they get results. Sadly, though, they still fall short of their full potential. The infighting, jockeying for position, and efforts spent covering oneself take precious energy and attention from achieving ever greater success.

Why Do NICE Teams Go FIERCE?

NICE teams start by accepting seven common myths about FIERCE teamwork that they believe will counter the NICE myths that they find don't always work for them:

Myth 1: *We don't need to lavish a lot of unnecessary praise on each other.*

We don't waste time and energy buttering ourselves up with positive feedback. We don't need that. We're good, and we know we're good. We don't need to be told. Constructive feedback and developmental feedback are what teams need, not positive reinforcement. Teams are all about improvement, not maintaining the status quo. Everyone loves working with such a helpful, supportive bunch of people!

The Sad Truth: We share only part of the story with each other. Our criticism is sharp and cutting. We constantly try to "fix" each other with feedback that is critical of how the job is being done. There's always a better way, and we look smart and show our value by being able to point that out to our peers. Giving positive feedback to others gives them an advantage we don't want to concede.

We don't help each other improve. Our negative feedback is so biting that the receivers react by dismissing it or by defending themselves. We rationalize that our harsh feedback is required to toughen up other team members. No wimps here! Everyone should be able to take it as well as dish it out. Particularly hurtful feedback prompts the receiver to eventually get even with the other person. Payback is inevitable. And when positive feedback is given, it is viewed as a weakness on the part of the giver, who thus gives an advantage to a peer (and competitor). Or the feedback is vague and has no real meaning other than as a pacifier. Or it's given to make the giver look good—a real "team player."

Myth 2: *We stay focused on the task and don't get sidetracked by talking about things that aren't directly work related.*

Being focused and goal-driven gets us results. We don't let people problems get in the way of results. We make good plans and then implement well. We are quick to take action!

The Sad Truth: We're so quick to take action, we rarely pause to anticipate problems. When problems *do* happen, we spring into action. We recognize and celebrate firefighters much more than we do planners who prevent the problems from happening in the first place. Some problems are people related, but we never seem to want to address those in advance. We'd rather wait for them to happen, solve them in the moment, and later complain about how inept, needy, or stupid those people can be!

Seemingly flawless plans can run into problems and roadblocks along the way. Rather than hold each other accountable, we look for scapegoats to blame. Problem solvers are revered. Planners are presumed guilty. Team members need to be quick to stay with the rest of the team. If you don't follow, just be quiet and go along with the group. Obviously the rest of us are smart enough to lead the effort, so you just trust us and fall in line. Don't let the team know you are not getting it: This will make you look weak and vulnerable.

Myth 3: *Our clients love us because we always find a way to get the job done.*

We're not here to give excuses. It may be tough, but we'll find a way to hit our goals. Anything to succeed!

The Sad Truth: We take on more work than we probably should, because we want to be successful. We are all committed to getting results, but disagree strongly on how to accomplish that. Power struggles follow as we sort out priorities, resources, and work responsibilities.

We work long and hard to hit deadlines, but the results come with consequences. Overwork, excessive overtime, and burnout are common on our team. We trust that the end justifies the means. Hitting a deadline is excuse enough to cut corners, relax standards, and step on toes. Almost anything is allowed to meet a deadline. We tell ourselves that we'll sort things out internally later, after we meet the goal. But we never do because we move on to the next task. We jockey for plum jobs or for work with high visibility. Real conflict erupts over prioritizing work, allocating resources, and getting key work assignments.

Myth 4: *We respect each other and the strengths each member brings to the team.*

We leverage our collective talents. We trust each other to make decisions for the good of the team and/or for the success of our efforts.

The Sad Truth: We are overly decisive. We don't wait for the green light from our boss or our peers if the decision doesn't directly affect them. It's easier to ask forgiveness than to get permission, so we take action immediately. When we involve the group, our decisions are made after lively discussion and arguing. It usually comes down to a vote and the majority rules. We don't like it when team members move forward without us, but we have no qualms doing the same thing to them. When *we* do it, we have good reason. When *they* do it, we question their logic or motives.

We take pride in individual accountability. As long as the decision was a good one, we love to take credit. If not, however, we look to justify ourselves, blame others, or otherwise deflect fault. We quickly distance ourselves from team members in trouble or under pressure to perform (unless helping them will make us heroes). We give cursory, insincere credit to the team when it succeeds, but the real credit goes to the individuals who did the main work. Jealousy over who's getting credit runs rampant.

Myth 5: *We refrain from conflict and drama.*

There's no place here for squabbling and pettiness. We all have a job to do, and we just do it. Everyone gets along so that we can get the job done.

The Sad Truth: We comfortably address differences of opinion about how the work should get done, but we rarely speak to problems we have dealing with each other. We expect individuals to work through any conflict by themselves. We see little value in talking about our conflict. This just takes time and energy that could (and should) be used to get the job done. Besides, we don't view this as real work anyway. We minimize relationship issues by calling them "drama." We assume that conflict is caused by immaturity or a lack of basic people skills. These things should be handled quickly and efficiently *offline* so that they don't get in the way of the real work.

We never resolve real problems, so they keep coming back to haunt us. We work around people issues so that we don't have to deal with them. We create alliances that are inefficient but that protect us from the alternative: conflict resolution. Alliance building creates extra steps and extra work for us, but it's preferable to dealing with the conflict. We know how to do work. So we view the extra work as just work, and accept it on top of everything else on our plates.

Myth 6: *We are focused and results oriented.*

Once we set our course, we are tenacious in our approach. Deadlines mean something to us, and we always hit them. We make plans and follow them faithfully. We don't get distracted by tangents, what-ifs, or nice-to-haves. We all know our roles, and we contribute to our collective success.

The Sad Truth: Once we make a decision, we are firm.
New information doesn't change our original plan. Too many egos are at stake to deviate just because we have new information that *may* affect the outcome. Unless the evidence is overwhelming, we stay doggedly resolute on our original approach. Flexibility is not our hallmark (unless we'll be recognized and rewarded for being flexible). Our discussions are linear, sequential, and controlled. We have no patience for tangents, sidebars, or related topics. Our meetings are quick and to the point. We share information, make decisions. and

then adjourn. No need to ponder or explore because we already know what to do and how to do it.

We stick to strict roles and responsibilities. Everyone has her or his part and had better come through. When something is missed, we look for someone to blame. If something falls through the cracks, we fix the process so that there are no cracks the next time. We don't look at how a more flexible approach may have helped us. Flexibility requires us to cooperate more, and we are better at individualizing the work and just doing our own parts. The plan is responsible for making sure all our parts add up to the desired whole. Once a decision is made, it's made. We don't rethink or reconsider unless there is overwhelming evidence that we have to. Even then, we are reluctant, and we start by first assigning blame to whoever messed up and now requires us to go back (inefficiently) and redo something. We protect our own turf and often build alliances to protect ourselves and/or each other.

Myth 7: *We are efficient.*

We don't waste time talking about feelings and emotions. We focus on the task, not on each other. When interpersonal relationship issues come up, we move to resolve them as quickly as possible so that they don't get in the way of the real work we're doing.

The Sad Truth: We brush over real interpersonal problems in the name of efficiency. When members try to address interpersonal issues, the rest of us hush them. We want to stay focused on the task at hand and use our time efficiently on the work, not on relationships. A cry for help or a request for support is seen as a sign of weakness. We expect relationships to take care of themselves. People shouldn't have to be coddled. After all, we don't want the people needs to get in the way of the real work.

We believe we're being efficient, but in reality we're not. We are working with limits created by our unwillingness to deal with our people issues. Being so task focused, we see only the work. We don't see how our team dynamics create work for us and keep us from being truly efficient. We waste time and energy working *around* issues instead of resolving them and creating a significant advantage for ourselves. We don't get it. We don't *want* to get it. We miss huge opportunities to leverage our potential synergy.

How FIERCE Teams Affect Their Members

When NICE teams go FIERCE, the same nine NICE team members have their same nine goals. They behave differently in a FIERCE environment, but they still strive to fulfill their personal desires.

The Peacemaker

The Peacemaker's goal of harmony and unity does not seem to be consistent with the FIERCE team's culture. FIERCE teams view a harmonious team as one that is not dealing with the real issues. Otherwise there would be arguments. Disagreement and discord are hallmarks of the FIERCE team.

Teammates openly attack one another. Tension, hostility, and fighting may abound.

In such a setting, the Peacemaker becomes overwhelmed with anxiety. What teammates call "just being honest" the Peacemaker sees as a personal attack and unnecessarily mean-spirited. Her natural optimistic approach turns negative. Ironically, the FIERCE team misinterprets her growing pessimism as a newfound realistic attitude and applauds it. She becomes more indecisive and even stubborn. The FIERCE team sees this as her standing her ground. So she is rewarded, at least initially, for her less than effective behaviors.

But then the FIERCE team responds with the very thing she isn't ready for at all: pressure to act.

As a FIERCE team member, she prefers to be noncommittal during the storm. Being openly confronted is very troubling for her, and so she may acquiesce in the moment for the sake of peace and harmony. Later, however, she digs in stubbornly. Rather than confront people openly as others do, she becomes passive-aggressive. This tactic helps her maintain an illusion of peace, while allowing her to assert herself, albeit indirectly.

In this state, doubts fill her mind and she obsesses about worst-case scenarios. She is suspicious of others and questions their intentions. Eventually, the more passive she is, the more the rest of the team ignores her—thus infuriating her. Fears and even paranoia then drive her to action rather than sound judgment or strategy.

Obviously, she rarely lasts long in such a situation and chooses one of two common outs. She may seek sanctuary in a NICE team, where her harmony focus is celebrated, or she works herself into the role of mediator between warring parties on the FIERCE team. Rarely required to voice her own position (which she is often out of touch with, anyway), she helps others resolve their differences. By doing this, she is able to stay removed from the conflict, at the same time promoting the peace and harmony she so earnestly desires.

The Champion

The Champion's need for power and influence appears to agree favorably with the FIERCE team. FIERCE teams are all about being honest and direct, assertive and straightforward. The Champion comes by this naturally, but he takes it too far.

For the Champion, having influence usually means being in control. He has little patience for the weak, pretenders, and fools. He wastes no time and minces no words with them. Ditto for anyone who opposes him. A sharp comment or quick outburst is usually all it takes to get the upper hand. Once in charge, he can be like the proverbial bull in the china shop—unaware of his clumsy and hurtful impact on others.

He maintains power and control so that he doesn't have to expose his own weakness or vulnerability. But he also uses that power and control to protect anyone he deems worthy: a friend, an ally, or an underdog (anyone he feels is being treated unjustly).

The Champion insists on the truth. He erroneously believes that real honesty comes out only in an argument. So he thinks nothing of inciting controversy and conflict just to provoke his teammates into expressing their real opinions and feelings. He doesn't expect and doesn't even want everyone to agree with him. He just demands that they be honest and stand up for what they really believe. If they do, the Champion will respect them. He'd much rather respect a teammate than merely agree with one.

The FIERCE team encourages and rewards the Champion's aggressive behavior. He is held up to others as an example of being direct and straightforward. He accuses those not like him of being weak. The team mistakenly believes that the pain associated with his tactless and rude style is an unfortunate but very necessary by-product of a team requirement: honesty. So he blurts out whatever he wants and behaves however he wants, without regard for his impact on others. Asserting himself forcefully, he grabs the power necessary to be of great influence in the FIERCE team.

The Perfectionist

The Perfectionist's focus on high standards in pursuit of excellence complements the FIERCE team's values of quality and success. She is encouraged to be outspoken and direct.

The challenge for the Perfectionist comes when the FIERCE team is ready to sacrifice or compromise standards in an effort to find a shortcut to merely acceptable results. "Good enough" is never good enough for the Perfectionist, who resents this affront to her values and responds by digging in stubbornly. She judges others harshly (but probably not as harshly as she judges herself). In the FIERCE open and honest culture, she delivers sharp criticism freely. She doesn't hesitate to condemn others in public, private, or behind their backs. She may be pushy with her advice, or argumentative if anyone disagrees with her assessments. Her teammates feel nitpicked, disapproved of, or even flawed.

Indignant when her high expectations are not met, she may turn her anger inward and become depressed and despondent. She starts to blame herself. She loses trust in herself and second-guesses her approach. Self-pity consumes her. Her work slips as her self-confidence falters. Her teammates become justifiably critical of her as well, adding to her downward spiral.

As long as she and the team agree on (and stick to) performance standards, though, she is in her element as the champion of excellence. She will speak on behalf of quality. Her sharp eye for error, inconsistency, and shoddy work serves the FIERCE team well, while satisfying her own need for perfection.

The Energizer

The Energizer's focus is on options and enjoyment. The conflict and tension that come out of a FIERCE team culture may be especially unpleasant for the Energizer—if she's directly involved. If not, she may get sinful enjoyment from watching the fireworks! She may even be the instigator; if so, she quickly finds a clever way out when things get ugly.

Naturally a risk taker, the Energizer takes fewer risks in a FIERCE environment than on a NICE team. Multiple options quickly melt into just two: right and wrong, good and bad. With so obvious a choice, she becomes rigid and autocratic in her approach. The FIERCE team misinterprets this as the Energizer's getting serious and taking charge. They respond by pushing back—directly. This is the very kind of unpleasant conflict that the Energizer likes to avoid.

Her optimism is replaced by cynicism. She nitpicks and criticizes her teammates, all in the name of helping them be more effective or more productive. She knows the way: if only they would listen to her. Though she freely dishes out the criticism, she doesn't want to hear it. She resents feeling victimized by their criticism, especially when they criticize her plans and ideas. She responds by blaming others and deflecting accountability. Her quick thinking can leave teammates feeling like they are slow or unimaginative or that she is a know-it-all.

The high energy of the FIERCE team keeps the Energizer's interest, though. Quick-witted, she is able to fend for herself and usually can stay out of the crossfire. She is in her element when the team needs to create strategies or plans. She is most comfortable arguing future plans and strategies because she is able to think on so many levels at once. Her creative approach to work allows her to offer unusual or innovative solutions to the conflict around her. As long as she can stand clear of direct conflict, she is engaged and contributes options and playfulness to the team.

The Guardian

The Guardian's focus on trust and security is not something a FIERCE team culture fosters. So the Guardian creates alliances with select teammates for safety's sake. He quickly separates them into two groups: us and them, those he can trust and those he cannot. When one of "us" is attacked, he will jump to the member's defense. The FIERCE team misinterprets his defensiveness as healthy debate and good argument. For the Guardian, however, the "attacker" becomes his enemy. He is much less concerned with the topic than he is with the relationship he has with the person he is defending or opposing. But since relationships are not dealt with in FIERCE teams, he continues to couch the conflict in terms of the task.

His need for safety prevents him from taking risks. Voicing an unpopular position invites strong pushback, maybe even personal attacks from teammates. Asking unpopular questions makes you a target. Pointing out the downside of an idea opens you up to special scrutiny. For the most part, he lets go of his role as devil's advocate, even though the FIERCE team welcomes controversy. He rarely risks having to stand alone on a topic. But when he does challenge others, his questions come across as though he is cross-examining them. The FIERCE team mistakes his focus on potential danger as a bad attitude but appreciates the lively discussion prompted by his pessimism.

FIERCE teams have no tolerance for failure. There is no "learning from our mistakes." Success is paramount. Less than perfect, the Guardian does whatever he must to protect himself, even if it means bending the truth at times. On the surface he shows himself to be a dedicated, hardworking teammate. But inside he is afraid—even frozen.

The FIERCE culture pushes him into overdrive or manic "doing." Not necessarily productive, he finds security in just being busy and purportedly contributing. He keeps busy to avoid drawing attention to himself. Out of the spotlight, he finds the security he needs to stay engaged.

The Observer

The Observer's focus on information and objectivity fits nicely in the FIERCE culture, where information is power. The Observer is a natural collector of information and has true power. She hoards data and uses it for her own purposes. She withholds information to achieve her goals. The FIERCE team misinterprets this as arrogance or secretiveness. As a know-it-all, she makes her teammates feel irrational, overly emotional, or not very bright.

Unfortunately, her need for more and more information before taking action immobilizes her. When she *does* take action, it's sometimes done without having thought through the implications or consequences. She may act on unrealistic and unfounded hopes or optimism.

The FIERCE team conflict can distract her logic and thinking. She may take on new projects or commitments impulsively, just to get away from the team and its squabbles. Her rapid flow of ideas can get dizzying, even for her. The FIERCE team sees this behavior and loses confidence in her intellect.

The Observer is happy that FIERCE teams do not value the social connections typically required by a NICE team. She is more comfortable with the isolation she can create for herself on a FIERCE team. She engages in the conflict with outrage only after being severely provoked. But normally, she observes the realness of the team conflict without participating directly. She rarely even takes sides in a quarrel. She may see a potential solution to the situation, but sadly she stays quiet. She coolly observes and analyzes—reserving her objectivity.

The Individualist

The Individualist's focus is on individual expression and being unique. The FIERCE team culture promotes individuality. The Individualist is encouraged to speak up and speak out, and he does so quite comfortably.

But the Individualist's frame of reference tends to be his feelings, something FIERCE teams will pooh-pooh. Facts and figures matter, not feelings. His efforts to express any emotion is met with harsh resistance or even criticism. FIERCE teams don't have the time or the patience for anything as subjective and as ill defined as an emotion. If you can't see it, feel it, or count it, it doesn't warrant attention. The Individualist attempts to make the team human, and the FIERCE team responds with contempt. If he speaks up more fervently, they eventually concede, but only temporarily.

Because of his personal convictions, the Individualist has no qualms about engaging with others in a spirited debate, discussion, or even an argument about the work. He holds his own when disagreed with or even attacked. Being the lone dissenter in the group is not only comfortable for him, it affords him a secret sense of pride for sticking up for his ideals, even though he is alone in the fight.

The Individualist's creative nature means that he has insights that others miss. He can't help but approach work differently than they do. His original approach and his imagination make for results that are unique, beautiful, or astounding. He stands out (and loves that he does). FIERCE teams love the attention that he brings the team. They may fight over the kudos, though. After all, it was a *team* effort!

The Achiever

The Achiever's focus on results is quite consistent with the FIERCE team culture. She resists dealing with the emotional baggage others may want to bring to a team setting. She feels that any conflict should be dealt with quickly and decisively—with clear winners and losers.

Given her overcompetitiveness on the FIERCE team, everything becomes a win/lose proposition for the Achiever. "Win at all cost" is her mantra, and she rarely loses. The FIERCE culture doesn't foster a team player mentality. It's every person for herself, and in this environment the competitive Achiever usually comes out on top.

Image conscious, she is sensitive to criticism or blame. When faced with failure, she feels the victim of circumstances. She can be superficial and is not beyond using dishonesty or deception to look good if necessary.

The FIERCE team greatly values her productivity. While rewarding the success, members also condemn her individualistic approach. To them, it seems self-serving. She rejects their FIERCE feedback and criticism. Never one to concede failure, she sidesteps, denies, or defends herself against it. If she gets overwhelmed, she strikes out passive-aggressively at those who make her see her shortcomings. She can even lose sight of her goals and become less effective when under great pressure. She will respond by compulsively taking on even more work or by running in circles just to stay busy. This reaction can make her even less productive and lead her into a downward spiral of more work and less productivity until she burns out.

Achievers love that FIERCE teams don't waste time dealing with emotional baggage. They are major champions of the FIERCE team's focus on the task, the goal, and the objective. She's in her element when the discussions stay task focused and results oriented. Building a strategy, creating a game plan, and developing an implementation approach all exhilarate her. Working with the team to reach the goals is her greatest thrill.

The Helper

The Helper's attention is on his teammates. In the FIERCE culture, he sees their hurt and pain and works to help or protect the vulnerable or injured. His teammates can start to feel smothered by his good intentions. When push comes to shove, he redoubles his efforts and may come across as manipulative.

His kind, caring attitude turns to irritability and frustration at the lack of compassion shown by teammates toward each other, as well as to himself. He blames others for injustices. He makes demands to correct power imbalances (but is careful to align with the *real* power, if balance is not feasible). He browbeats others to get his way. Disappointed that others aren't caring for him the way he is for them, the gloves come off and he's ready to battle anyone to get things done.

When confronted, he backs down quickly (to avoid hurting others), or he is surprisingly sharp and aggressive in his response. He can be blunt, even rude, when he feels it's necessary to lay down the law. The Helper may argue or bully others to get his way successfully. Unaccustomed to being treated this way by him, his teammates back down.

In the FIERCE environment, where task is king, relationships are minimized. The Helper is the champion of the team's people needs. FIERCE teams may accept the need to address relationship issues, but they view it as something to be "done," almost like an item on a to-do list. The Helper usually volunteers for or gets assigned this "task." The FIERCE team doesn't much value this role. Nevertheless, it allows the Helper to satisfy his need to help and care for others, whether or not they really need (or even want) it.

FIERCE Team Norms

Put all nine of these team members in a FIERCE environment, and you get a different set of team norms from those of a NICE team. NICE team players quickly adapt, as just described.

On the surface, each FIERCE team player openly condemns FIERCE team behaviors. They claim they want the team to address the needs of the team members, not just focus on the task. But they refrain from doing so as long as there is pressure to perform. No one wants to be the first to throw a wrench into the machinery that is (on the surface) working so smoothly. They won't take precious time or effort away from making the numbers just to address people issues. That's too risky!

Can these FIERCE team members be effective? Of course they can. They just don't reach their full potential in such a setting. They remain complacent, adjusting to the FIERCE environment. At least for now, adjusting is safer and more comfortable than what they see as the "obvious" alternative of going back to being a NICE team. So:

- The Peacemaker accepts the role of mediator to promote harmony, but without getting personally involved.

- The Champion bludgeons the team with brutal honesty, without regard for the impact on team members.

- The Perfectionist resents compromises to quality, without holding the team accountable for its indulgences.

- The Energizer bullies the team into accepting innovation, without its being much fun for anyone.

- The Guardian forges subteam alliances to create pockets of security, without addressing whole team needs.

- The Observer uses information recklessly, without thinking through the implications of her actions.

- The Individualist marches to his own beat, without leveraging the team members' collective potential.

- The Achiever loses focus as she tries to do it all, without regard for the personal damage left behind.

- The Helper takes on the role of relationship soother, without taking care of his own needs.

Commitment to the FIERCE team is typically not very high. A look-out-for-number-one mentality prevails. Team members accept and even encourage independent (rather than *interdependent*) team roles. They may be aware of their team's potential, but they don't believe they can attain that potential. NICE didn't work, so the opposite should work, right? They'd never guess that being "not so FIERCE" might be part of the answer.

So if being FIERCE isn't the answer, and if NICE isn't the answer either, what is? The answer is BOLD.

Summary

▫ The opposite of NICE teams are FIERCE teams. NICE teams go FIERCE in the belief that FIERCE will deliver them from the problems of being NICE.

▫ FIERCE teams are stuck in the storming stage of team development, unwilling or unable to move through this stage to become higher performing on the other side.

▫ Typically, when FIERCE doesn't work, teams retreat to NICE.

▫ There are seven myths of FIERCE teams, all of which promise false benefits and neglect the damaging consequences:

1. It's unnecessary to praise each other (and only criticism is helpful).
2. Avoid everything not directly related to the task (and don't anticipate problems).

3. Clients love our ability to get things done (and we suffer from burnout).

4. Individual team member strengths are valued (and they may take on the team's accountability single-handedly).

5. Avoid conflict or drama (and do more work to avoid any real problems).

6. Focus on results (and neglect what the team members need).

7. Prize efficiency (and then ignore it again with work-arounds).

○ The nine types of FIERCE team players are NICE team players who have various reasons for coping in the FIERCE team environment:

1. The Peacemaker focuses on harmony (while becoming overwhelmed by conflict).

2. The Champion focuses on influence (while fighting with anyone and everyone).

3. The Perfectionist focuses on excellence and quality (while resenting shortcuts to "acceptable" results).

4. The Energizer focuses on enjoyment (while taking fewer risks).

5. The Guardian focuses on trust and security (while separating the team into "us" and "them").

6. The Observer focuses on information and objectivity (while withholding information).

7. The Individualist focuses on uniqueness (while long-ing for what isn't).

8. The Achiever focuses on success (while winning at all costs).

9. The Helper focuses on supporting others (while blam-ing others for injustices).

◘ The very things that FIERCE team members seek are the things that elude them as they play too FIERCEly together.

♦ ♦ ♦

**You have enemies? Good. That means you've
stood up for something some time in your life.**
Winston Churchill

3

The Sweet Spot Between NICE and FIERCE: BOLD

Be who you are and say what you feel because those who mind don't matter and those who matter don't mind.

Dr. Seuss

NICE teams are too NICE. FIERCE teams are too FIERCE. They are just two extremes of the same team continuum. The sweet spot in the middle is BOLD. BOLD teams balance NICE's compassion, consideration, and caring with FIERCE's courage, risk taking, and honesty. The balance is a delicate one, and it doesn't come easily.

BOLD teams realize that it's not just *what* they do that's

important: It's *how* they do it, too. *What* they do gives them the short-term success. *How* they do it sets them up for future success, through growth and development. BOLD team members won't sacrifice an investment in the long run for a short-term win. The *what* and *how* are interdependent. BOLD teams can't excel in one area without being mindful of the other. The team's accomplishments are greater when members tend to each other's needs. Their relationships are stronger when they tend to the task.

BOLD teams effectively move past the *forming* and *storming* stages of team development into *norming,* and even on to *performing*.

Why BOLD Teams Are More Successful Than NICE or FIERCE Teams

BOLD teams know that success is about balance. They understand that spending too much time and energy protecting each other's feelings (NICE) has a cost. They also know that spending too much time and energy on the task (FIERCE) also has a cost. They strike a balance between the realities of NICE and FIERCE teams to create a new, BOLD reality.

Truth 1: *We give each other balanced feedback.*

Like FIERCE teams, we realize that constructive feedback is critical for our improvement but that it doesn't have to be harsh to be helpful. We are direct, honest, and straightforward with each other. Our criticism comes from a place of caring and a sincere desire to help each other. We *offer* constructive feedback because we deliver it in a truly helpful way. We trust that our teammates will receive our feedback in the spirit in which it is offered. And, we actively *seek* constructive feedback from our teammates because we trust they will offer information that will help us improve.

As with NICE teams, positive feedback is important for reinforcing great behavior. We motivate each other by recognizing effective behaviors so that our teammates know what's working and what isn't. But we avoid vague, empty platitudes. Instead, we are as deliberate, specific, and forthcoming with positive feedback as we are with developmental feedback. We elaborate. We give details and examples. And we don't hesitate to ask each other for positive feedback either. There's no shame in needing—and asking for—positive reinforcement now and then.

Truth 2: *We pay attention to the work itself, as well as how we work.*

We are conscientious about results. The reason we exist as a team is to deliver. We work hard to hit deadlines, conserve precious resources, and get the job done well. We prioritize our time and resources to meet the expectations set for us as well as our own commitments. But time lines and goals don't drive us. We drive them—or at least we manage them.

We take the time to challenge our assumptions about not only what work *should* be done, but also *how* we should do it. We want to consider all viewpoints before firming up our plans and heading into implementation. Our goal is to hear from everyone before proceeding, so we actively solicit input from quieter teammates.

We especially welcome the devil's advocate type of discussions. We consider potential problems, not just potential payoffs. This approach helps us build preventive measures into our plans so that we can avoid most problems. It also helps us plan our contingent actions up front so that we are ready if a problem does arise. We are more effective if we're ready for obstacles than when we are caught off guard and shoot from the hip.

Truth 3: *We balance our desire to say "yes" with the reality of resources and competing priorities.*

We are not in business to say "no." We want to say "yes" to each request made of us. Although it feels good to do so, we also know the dangers of overextending ourselves. And we recognize that our organization has entrusted us with valuable resources. It's our job, as stewards of our time, budget dollars, and other resources, to be responsible to the whole organization, not just to ourselves or clients or partners who may happen to be our favorites.

Before accepting work, we *realistically* assess our ability to deliver. We have frank discussions about our current workload, sharing concerns and reservations as well as hopes and desires. The merits of incoming work are weighed against what we've already committed to doing. We avoid putting ourselves in the position of overwork or burnout because in the long run that serves no one's needs.

We don't want new priorities to overshadow prior commitments either. So we reprioritize only when it is absolutely necessary. Even then, we check in with our partners before making changes to time lines or resource allocations that may affect them. We use "no" sparingly and only when we have solid, fair, and logical evidence for saying it. When we do have to decline work, we offer our partners alternatives to help them still achieve their goals, but perhaps in different ways.

Truth 4: *We respect the diversity of experience and approach on the team.*

Decisions are made with everyone's input and participation. By respecting each other's experience and expertise, we avoid dismissing the perspective that others on the team may have. Newcomers and those without direct bearing on a specific issue still have valuable input for us. They can see things that those of us in the thick of it miss. They ask the "stupid" questions that only those not in the know can ask. These are often the most helpful questions for us to address!

We don't expect any one team member to make a decision for the team on his or her own—not even our leader. Shared accountability leads to the team's success. We know that being part of the decision-making process means that each individual will commit more wholeheartedly to the result than if a decision is given to (or forced upon) us. By deciding together, we are more accountable to each other. Even though one of us may take the lead on something, the rest of us are right there in support to ensure *our* success.

There are no winners and losers on issues. We all win together or lose together. Because it's all collective, we work all the harder to ensure the wins.

Truth 5: *We encourage healthy debate.*

Conflicts are addressed as they come up. We realize that conflict is part of any healthy relationship and that unresolved conflict becomes a cancer in a group. By not shying away from conflict, we make ourselves more mutually vulnerable. We share our honest reactions. We express how we think or feel, as well as what we want or need from each other. Everyone is encouraged to be transparent and genuine.

However, we don't lash out at each other when we feel hurt or offended. We approach conflict with compassion. We trust each other. Conflict presents an opportunity to resolve issues and actually strengthen our working relationships, not a way to get back at someone. As a result, conflict is not unnecessary "drama." Dealing with our conflict is just as much a part of our real work as meeting deadlines.

We strive to remove obstacles to working effectively *together.* By not accepting Band-Aids, we stick with a conflict until we all feel confident that it has been resolved. Understanding that we are dealing with our imperfect and unpredictable humanness makes us patient and forgiving as we work toward true and lasting resolution.

Truth 6: *We balance our need to plan with our need to be flexible.*

Like FIERCE teams, we make plans. We scope out projects and make budgets, forecasts, action plans, and work assignments. But we draw on *all* our collective experience and wisdom to plan ideal courses of action because this is the best way to manage toward better results. We don't rely on just a few to decide for us: We put all our cards on the table. We have open and frank discussions about what is possible, given various other demands and constraints. Then we decide together.

Since everyone is part of creating the plan, each of us is involved and understands the ins and outs of our work. This allows us to be flexible when we need to be. We don't get distracted with tangents and nice-to-haves when we know what is truly important and why. While focused on the plan, we can make intelligent, quality choices if it makes sense to deviate from our original position for one reason or another. Plans are treated as just what they are: *plans*. They are not edicts or commandments. We address unique opportunities or obstacles, as they arise, with appropriate flexibility.

Meetings are no different. We have agendas and, for the most part, stick to them. But we are flexible enough to realize that sometimes we need to veer, perhaps because the agenda was flawed or something unexpected and important came up. We make sure the change is for good reason, not just a way to avoid something unpleasant or unpopular. And the team—not an individual—makes the decision to change course. Adjusting an agenda midway through a meeting doesn't throw us. We also consider how we'll eventually address the rest of the agenda before we go off of it for something else.

Truth 7: *We are efficient in both the short and the long term.*

Short-term results are important; so we drive for them. Our focus is on getting the job done, on time and within budget.

We know that many assess our success by what we have ac-complished lately. But we also won't sacrifice the future for the present. If issues come up now, continually putting them off because we don't have time today doesn't serve us well. Sometimes it makes sense to stop and regroup before moving forward. This gives us renewed vigor and a sense of purpose.

If we find ourselves creating work-arounds or altering our approach to accommodate internal obstacles, we call this out and deal with it. Although it slows us down momentarily, fully addressing—and resolving—team problems *now* means that we won't have to work around them again. And again. Investing effort now can pay off in a big way later on, so we don't get bent out of shape when people have a fear, a fit, or a feeling that they need to share. Rather than labeling them as troublemakers or weak or whiners, we celebrate their braveness and jump in with them to address and resolve the problem at hand.

How BOLD Team Members Interact So Successfully

You'll find the same people on BOLD teams as you do on NICE and FIERCE teams. But they behave differently here, because they can more fully realize their potential.

The Peacemaker

The Peacemaker, with her focus on team harmony, unity, and peace, shuns conflict as a member of either a NICE or a

FIERCE team. She sees peace and conflict as incompatible. On a NICE team, she encourages others to avoid conflict all together: "Let's all play nice here!" If the team can't avoid conflict, she helps minimize it: "Come on, it's not that big a deal!" On a FIERCE team, she denies her own position and her own role in any conflict: "No, I said I'm fine!" She distracts herself by mediating others' conflict instead. She gets caught up in trying to resolve all their conflicts—as if that is actually possible.

On a BOLD team, however, she accepts the view of peace and conflict held by Dorothy Thompson (the first American journalist expelled from Nazi Germany): "Peace is not the absence of conflict, but the presence of creative alternatives for responding to conflict—alternatives to passive or aggressive responses, alternatives to violence."

So the Peacemaker on the BOLD team confronts her teammates directly. Her talent to see all sides of an issue helps her respect all perspectives and those who hold the different opinions. She confronts team members in a way that maintains their dignity and self-esteem. It's a peaceful conflict, neither passive nor aggressive.

Fully present, the Peacemaker focuses her attention better on a BOLD team. She is more in touch with what is truly important to her. That ability empowers her to take action. She takes the lead more. She invites collaboration, rather than waiting for it merely to happen. And she speaks up: even at the risk of stating a position or opinion that may conflict with someone else's. Her fortitude inspires others to dare speak, too.

The Peacemaker believes that BOLD provides team

members with true peace and harmony based on an unconditional regard and appreciation for each other. It does.

The Champion

As a member of either a NICE or a BOLD team, the Champion, with his focus on power and influence, tries to exert influence over the team and its work. He invites pushback so that he can deal with it head-on. On a NICE team, however, there is no pushback. So he bites his tongue to avoid alienation: "No objections? Great, let's move on." He'll push for action as soon as he feels he can get away with it: "How about if I just get this started while you're figuring out the details?" On the FIERCE team, he's a force to be reckoned with: "Well, that's just not going to work. So let's do it my way instead!" He makes a grab for power and continues to go after more. Brutal honesty provides a release for him, even though it may harm his teammates.

On a BOLD team, however, the Champion's bias for truth serves him and the team equally well. He runs contrary to Voltaire's complaint, "One of the chief misfortunes of honest people is that they are cowardly." Courageous above all else, the Champion fosters candid speech on the BOLD team. Unafraid of doing it wrong but being careful not to step on toes, he calls out the elephants in the room and persuades the rest of the team to acknowledge and deal with them before they move on.

Energetic and passionate, he's quite comfortable being the lone voice of opposition to an idea, opinion, or even the status quo. He may singlehandedly prevent the team from settling into mediocrity or complacency. He may also single-handedly propel the team to action they never thought possible. He uses his power for the good of all.

He's a natural leader on the BOLD team, even if he doesn't have the title. Others follow him because of his example. Gone are the things that made him intimidating on a FIERCE or even a NICE team. Here, the Champion wears his heart on his sleeve and, by so doing, reveals his own vulnerability. He's more accessible, more approachable, and more caring. He attracts cooperation and has greater impact through his efforts.

The Champion believes that BOLD offers opportunity for true and lasting positive influence. It does.

The Perfectionist

As a member of either a NICE or FIERCE team, the Perfectionist, concerned with the pursuit of excellence, promotes quality at every turn. Nothing ever seems good enough. On a NICE team, she is the quality monitor: "That's not quite right!" Her narrow focus tends to see options only in pairs: right and wrong, good and bad. She misses all the gray. On a FIERCE team, the Perfectionist can be judgmental and harsh: "You're wrong . . . again!" She will retreat inwardly and blame herself for the imperfections that plague her. She'll also beat herself up unnecessarily for the imperfections of the team.

On a BOLD team, however, the Perfectionist embraces imperfection. She concedes, "Being happy doesn't mean that everything is perfect. It means you've decided to look beyond the imperfections." (And how wonderfully imperfect is it that this is the only quote in the book whose author is unknown?)

The Perfectionist accepts that even imperfection can be perfect. She releases her insistence on absolutes and opens herself to accepting anything and everything that occurs. She speaks from a place of moral and ethical conviction, but with an appreciation of her teammates differing, yet equally valid convictions.

She adapts a positive outlook and shifts her attitude away from what's bad toward what's good. Affirming and enthusiastic, she sees complex options where others may see only black and white. She is natural and spontaneous as she genuinely enjoys her team membership. Her openness and optimism are contagious, and she helps the team to accomplish bigger and better things.

The Perfectionist believes that BOLD advances purposeful excellence and quality. It does.

The Energizer

Primarily concerned with innovation and enjoyment, the Energizer tries to keep things upbeat and positive on a NICE or a FIERCE team. She sees disagreement as a threat to her fun and as a limit to her options. On a NICE team, she works to keep things light and cheery: "Let's all have fun here!" If that's unsuccessful, she scolds them: "Hey, it's only work, don't be so serious!" On a FIERCE team, she limits hers (and others') thinking to safe, not so controversial ideas and options. Conflict is minimized and agreement is more likely that way: "The answer is sooooo obvious here, folks!" She steers clear of direct involvement in conflict (which would be unpleasant) but may sit back and be entertained by the "show" if others get into it.

On a BOLD team, however, her creativity and enthusiasm can blossom. She accepts Oscar Wilde's challenge: "An idea that is not dangerous is unworthy to be called an idea at all." Free to explore dreams, the Energizer leads the team on visionary adventures. Ideas, opinions, and perspectives are all shared and explored openly and fairly. Her natural curiosity prompts the team to remain open and objective long after they normally would have shut down. She leads them to find unique solutions to even the most routine of problems.

BOLD planning leads to action for the Energizer. She focuses her mental energy not just on what *could* be, but *how*. She slows down and commits to real priorities. Real action. She sticks with the task and follows through to completion. She reconciles the pleasant with the not-so-pleasant, and she lives a fuller, more "real" experience. Her passion for constant stimulation gives way to a feeling of being complete and satisfied. Her commitment inspires others to stay equally dedicated and focused.

The Energizer believes that BOLD encourages unlimited opportunity for innovation, creativity, and downright fun. It does.

The Guardian

As a member of either NICE or FIERCE teams, the Guardian, focusing on trust and security, seeks safety for himself first and for the team second. He is suspicious of others and their ulterior motives. On a NICE team, he remains on guard: "Why—really—is he saying that?" When a decision is made, he second-guesses it immediately: "We should have considered this point more carefully!" On a FIERCE team, he accepts work beyond his capacity to function well. He keeps excessively busy to avoid drawing the same scrutiny to himself that he doles out to others: "No problem, I'll take care of that . . . too!" He mistrusts most of his teammates but creates alliances with a limited few for power and protection.

On a BOLD team, however, he finds his inner authority and speaks out. Maggie Kuhn (founder of the Gray Panthers) encourages the Guardian: "Speak your mind—even if your voice shakes." So the Guardian conquers his fears in the safe environment of a BOLD team. He accepts that his devil's advocate voice is invaluable to the team's success and shares it liberally. The team welcomes his realistic perspective and pauses to consider threats before rushing headlong into possible disaster.

The Guardian puts his trust not only in himself but in his teammates. He takes a broader point of view, and that vantage point allows him to trust in more positive outcomes from all. By taking action that is well thought-out, he moves past his fears. He frees up energy, allowing himself to relax a bit (by not being so vigilant) and to enjoy the team experience more completely. His example eases tension on the team, promoting a more open, trusting environment.

The Guardian believes that BOLD creates safety and security for individuals as well as for the team. It does.

The Observer

As a member of either the NICE or FIERCE team, the Observer tries to remain detached, longing to have information to understand and to be objective. When the team shares information, she holds back. She may share only when called on. When she does, her comments are often sparse, and they may make her seem like she's trying to stay aloof: "Yes, I think that you have all made good points!" On FIERCE teams, she is pushed into acting without really thinking things through: "OK, I'm just going to do it and see what happens!" But she does so only if staying detached and removed doesn't work for her.

On the BOLD team, however, the Observer agrees with Johann Wolfgang von Goethe: "Knowing is not enough; we must apply. Willing is not enough; we must do." So the Observer actually applies her knowledge, thinking, and understanding for the good of the BOLD team. In doing so, she gains even more insight—the kind that comes only from personal experience and involvement.

The Observer trusts her instincts when she is on a BOLD team, because taking risks is encouraged. She comes out of her shell to speak up and be heard. No longer hoarding information, she shares and is even willing to confront others, if necessary, to get things done. Her bias for action energizes others on the team and leads them toward the results they all seek.

The Observer believes that BOLD offers the ideal complement of insight and action. It does.

The Individualist

On a NICE or FIERCE team, the Individualist, concerned with uniqueness and self-expression, wants to express himself. He needs to feel like he is special and unique. On the NICE team, he tries to find his niche by helping others he has empathy for: "I know what you're going through. Here, let me take care of that for you." He thinks that, by helping others, they in turn will help him. He gets depressed when his teammates don't reciprocate. On a FIERCE team, his willingness to be authentic is appreciated and encouraged: "Here's how I feel . . ." But feelings aren't particularly valued by a FIERCE team, so he is dismissed as weak or soft. Only when he's as FIERCE as the others is he respected.

On a BOLD team, however, the Individualist can be an individual. Free to express his unique self, he's in agreement with Billie Holiday, "If I'm going to sing like someone else, then I don't need to sing at all." Speaking his piece means he can contribute to the team's success in his own way, without selling out or conforming. No one has to agree with him, just so long as he's heard and appreciated for his perspective.

More structured in his approach, the Individualist can balance his internal feelings with a clarity of vision and a greater precision in follow-through. He relies less on his inner emotion and finds grounding in his principles. Steady and realistic, he's able to do more problem solving and be more practical. He sees the positive as well as the negative. He appreciates what is, rather than what is missing. And he uses his creativity to find approaches and solutions that are inspired, imaginative, and out of the ordinary.

The Individualist believes that BOLD solidifies team purpose because of, not in spite of, individuality. It does.

The Achiever

While a member of either a NICE or FIERCE team, the Achiever, who is focused on productivity and results, wants to be (or at least look) successful. She confuses her image with her true self. On a NICE team she works hard to be successful and to look good: "No one's going to get in the way of me hitting our objectives!" She avoids even the appearance of failure, even if it means relaxing standards or crafting just the right angle for a message: "Let's just say this, instead: It'll fly!" On a FIERCE team, the Achiever leads the team to steamroll over people problems: "Why don't you guys take that offline so we can get back to work here?" When the pressure to perform intensifies, she works harder—but not necessarily smarter. Busyness becomes the mistaken focus in her desperate attempts to avoid failure (or the perception of it).

On a BOLD team, however, she lets go of her concern over how others perceive her. She learns, as Bill Cosby has, that "the key to failure is trying to please everybody." Having failure on the BOLD team is not the same as *being* a failure. She finds that she is valued and appreciated for who she is, not what she does or what she accomplishes.

The Achiever connects with her BOLD teammates. Feeling part of a "real team," she commits to the team's success, not just to her personal success. Trusting her teammates allows her to delegate or at least to let go of feeling that she has to do it all herself. She matches her natural optimism with realism. She respects that balancing her results orientation with a concern for the team and how it operates actually leads to consistently better results. Her trust in her teammates is infectious and spreads quickly, for even better bottom-line results.

The Achiever believes that BOLD means top-notch performance, no matter how you measure it. It does.

The Helper

As a member of either a NICE or FIERCE team, the Helper, who is all about his teammates and their needs, tries to keep everyone happy or at least feeling attended to. He is very in tune with what his teammates need. On a NICE team, he works to anticipate and then meet those needs: "We haven't heard from you yet, and I'm sure you have something important to say. Come on!" If conflict arises, he seeks to soothe both parties: "Janet, I think this is what Karen means to say!" On a FIERCE team, the Helper may take on the task of juggling everyone's relationships: "OK guys, can't we all try to be civil to each other?" When pressed, though, he alienates his teammates by issuing orders, bullying, and otherwise taking control to resolve a situation that warrants it. All in the name of helping others.

On a BOLD team, however, the Helper accepts that it's possible for a team to support both conflict and personal care appropriately. As Milton R. Sapirstein (a pioneer in psychoanalysis) puts it, "differing opinions need not imply an absence of love." The Helper models handling conflict in a compassionate and supportive way.

The Helper gets in touch with his own needs, without waiting for or expecting others to "read" him. This inward reflection helps him develop convictions that do not depend on others' opinions and thus are quite strong indeed.

He claims and acts on his own aspirations. He says "no" comfortably and without guilt. He expresses himself more creatively. Self-acceptance replaces a dependency on others for validation. Acknowledging himself and his own needs leads to a greater sense of autonomy and freedom. He finds new ways to bring value to the team. His independence motivates others to find their own voices and contribute to the team in unique and exciting ways.

The Caregiver believes that BOLD inspires camaraderie and independence at the same time. It does.

BOLD Team Norms

These nine people on a team can quickly move through the four stages of team development. *Storming* isn't as scary for the BOLD team as for NICE teams, nor does it take as long as NICE teams fear. It's a critical step on the BOLD team's journey toward *performing*.

Once in the *performing* stage, the team may cycle back through the earlier stages, especially when membership changes (someone joins or leaves the team). But these loop-backs are generally much quicker than the original journey. And each time the team emerges from a stage, it performs more strongly and effectively than ever.

On the BOLD team, the NICE team players have found

the perfect blend of caring for and about each other, and accomplishing job challenges and reaching goals together:

- The Peacemaker discovers that the real harmony on the other side of conflict is well worth the effort.
- The Champion has real influence when others' needs are addressed.
- The Perfectionist enjoys the real excellence that happens when perfection has so many options.
- The Energizer has great fun with the real enthusiasm that is grounded in reality.
- The Guardian relaxes in the real security that is experienced among trusted teammates.
- The Observer comes alive when the real objectivity gets put into action.
- The Individualist expresses real creativity that is rooted in principle.
- The Achiever celebrates the real success that comes from team synergy.
- The Caregiver sees the real needs of teammates expressed and met—including his or her own.

Commitment to the BOLD team is extremely high. Team members care deeply for—and about—each other. They support and strengthen one another, growing and learning together. They work through important conflict, emerging each time even more committed than before. Trust soars. Respect pervades. Collaboration reigns. They truly relish what NICE teams can only *pretend* to have.

BOLD teams accomplish the extraordinary. They consistently exceed expectations. They wow clients by always delivering on their promises. Together, they find ways to beat deadlines and come in under budget, *without* having padded either one to begin with. Visions become reality. Goals are surpassed. Excellence is achieved. They savor what FIERCE teams can only cross their fingers for.

Individually, members' participation on the BOLD team fills them with pride and satisfaction. They share the sentiment, "Wow, *this* is how a team should be!"

Three Requirements of All BOLD Team Members

As you may imagine, a BOLD team doesn't just happen; it takes a finesse that comes from a conscientious effort by each of its members. BOLD team members have in common three qualities that absolutely must be present for their team to flourish: caring, faith, and trust.

◻ Team members must *care* enough to put in the required effort. BOLD teams take hard work and energy. Team members who don't care, don't try. A handful of team members cannot carry the load for the rest of the team: BOLD teams require full participation. The energy to initiate BOLD or to preserve BOLD when the going gets tough (such as in the *storming* stage) comes from caring. Successful BOLD team members care about the work, and they care about each other.

◘ Team members must have *faith* and patience that their efforts will pay off. NICE behaviors are well established. They are comfortable, and team members feel secure in that comfort. It takes faith to believe that new behaviors will improve results. It takes faith to make BOLD worth trying in the first place. And it takes patience to stick with BOLD long enough to reap the benefits. BOLD teams don't just happen overnight: They require conviction and perseverance.

◘ Team members must *trust* themselves and each other. BOLD is built on open and honest communication. Speaking up takes courage. Courage comes from a confidence in yourself as well as in your teammates. It's risky. Those afraid to take such risks play it safe—that's NICE. Speaking out means mistakes are made. Toes are stepped on (inadvertently). Trusting forgives mistakes, assumes innocent motives, and refrains from judging others. BOLD teams share information freely, trusting it will be handled confidentially and without malice.

The Four BOLD Principles

The trick, then, is to turn this internal commitment into a shared BOLD reality. Teams do this by adhering to the four BOLD principles.

BOLD Principle 1: Assume innocence.

BOLD team members trust that each other's behaviors are born of innocence, not malice. They give each other the benefit of the doubt. They approach confrontation from a place of caring. They take the time and effort to plan not only how, but also where and when, they will confront each other before jumping in willy-nilly. They plan for success.

BOLD Principle 2: *Build a bridge.*

BOLD team members are considerate of each other. Before confronting a teammate, they first check their teammate's readiness. Then they lay the groundwork for a productive conversation by starting from a point of commonality or agreement. Of course, this works only when they have taken the time and energy to fully understand their teammate's position before launching into their own. Listening and sensitivity are key.

BOLD Principle 3: *Speak your truth.*

BOLD team members understand that perception is reality. In interpersonal relationships, there are no absolute truths. Team members share their own reality as specifically as possible with each other, avoiding generalizations, accusations, and misinterpretations. Confrontation is valid and justified (and worth the effort) as long as they can relate it to the organization's goals or priorities. Otherwise there's no real need to have the discussion.

BOLD Principle 4: *Invite dialogue.*

BOLD team members are curious about their colleagues' opinions and actively seek to hear them. They anticipate and prepare for a possible negative reaction to a confrontation. They are ready to find common ground and move to resolution, even if that means giving in a little (or a lot). *Winning* is not the goal, *resolution* is.

This is work—real work! Why bother?

BOLD teams are more effective and more fulfilling than NICE or FIERCE teams.

Summary

◘ NICE and FIERCE represent two ends of the team continuum; BOLD is the happy balance of the two.

◘ BOLD teams effectively move through the *forming* and *storming* stages of team development and find great success in *norming* and *performing*.

◘ There are seven truths of a BOLD team, all of which contribute to its overall success:

1. We give each other both positive (reinforcing) and constructive (developmental) feedback, so that it's truly balanced.

2. We pay attention to *how* we work together as well as to *what* we work on together.

3. We prioritize our workload so that we take on work responsibly.

4. We make decisions with respect for the diversity of our collective strengths.

5. We encourage healthy debate before deciding on a course of action.

6. We can balance our focus on results with our ability to adapt.

7. We are efficient in the short as well as in the long term.

◘ There are nine types of BOLD team members, each with a different reason for promoting the team:

1. The Peacemaker focuses on harmony (and finds it on the other side of healthy conflict).

2. The Champion focuses on influence (and finds it by empowering others).

3. The Perfectionist focuses on the "right" way (and finds it by considering multiple options).

4. The Energizer focuses on enjoyment (and finds it through hard work and focus).

5. The Guardian focuses on security (and finds it by letting go of worry).

6. The Observer focuses on understanding (and finds it through taking action).

7. The Individualist focuses on uniqueness (and finds it through order and discipline).

8. The Achiever focuses on success (and finds it by engaging the rest of the team).

9. The Helper focuses on others' needs (and meets them by including his or her own as well).

◘ All BOLD team members share three important qualities: they care, they believe, and they trust.

❑ BOLD team members realize their true desires on BOLD teams—personally and professionally—by practicing four principles:

1. Assume innocence.
2. Build a bridge.
3. Speak your truth.
4. Invite dialogue.

◆ ◆ ◆

This above all: to thine own self be true.

WILLIAM SHAKESPEARE

4

BOLD Principles

Conflict is inevitable, but combat is optional.

Max Lucado

NICE and FIERCE are at two ends of a spectrum. At one end we have ultra-NICE, where team members protect themselves and others from what they perceive to be the hurtful truth. At the other end we have ultra-FIERCE, where team members assert their raw truth regardless of the impact it may have on others. NICE overemphasizes (and coddles) people. FIERCE overemphasizes (and brutalizes) truth. BOLD lies in the middle, balancing *people* needs with *truth* needs. BOLD means truth is spoken, but in a humane, caring way. BOLD means people are protected, but they're not protected from the truth. They're protected from the hurtful or disrespectful ways the truth can be delivered. Figure 4–1 shows these relationships.

Figure 4-1. The NICE-BOLD-FIERCE continuum.

NICE	BOLD	FIERCE
◄───►		
Protect People (from the Pain of Truth)	Balance: Compassion and Courage (People Needs and Truth)	Assert Truth (Regardless of its Impact on People)

NICE team members dance around issues and don't speak what is real. They're afraid that saying what they really think or feel will hurt others. Or they worry that, by saying what is true to them, they might have to stand up and defend themselves. They might have to engage, and engagement takes energy that they don't want to exert. A NICE team member may be the only one who thinks a certain way, but standing alone can be frightening or cause conflict. It's much more comfortable to sit back and be quiet. Whitewashing the truth so that it comes out soft, sterile, or vague—so as not to cause offense or controversy—is also easier. The theme is one of cowardice: NICE team members lack the courage to stand up and be counted.

At the other extreme is FIERCE. Team members are so committed to the task that people issues take a backseat. Speaking the truth (to get the job done) is more important than worrying about others' feelings. FIERCE team members are more concerned with getting things off their chests and "out there" than anything else. Or they have to call out anyone who is trying to "get away with" something. They just blurt out what's on their minds, and let others worry about how to deal with it. The theme is, "My needs take precedence over yours." FIERCE team members lack the compassion or the consideration to craft their messages so they can be heard without the collateral damage that comes from an assault.

In the middle is BOLD. These team members are concerned not only with being open and honest, but also with how they come across to their teammates. They want to protect each other from hurt, but not at the expense of speaking the truth. They want to share truth with each other, but not at the expense of the relationship. They balance protecting people with asserting truth, simultaneously showing compassion and courage.

Figure 4–2 shows the NICE-BOLD-FIERCE continuum. To the left are examples of NICE statements. Toward the center, NICE gains courage and develops into BOLD. Further right, however, courage overwhelms compassion, and we decline into FIERCE. Notice that there are no clear cutoffs between the types of teams. The lines of differentiation are not exact or precise.

Most teams are not BOLD. They usually lean toward NICE or FIERCE, at either of the very ends of the continuum, favoring one extreme or the other. There may also be

Figure 4-2. Typical messages on the NICE-BOLD-FIERCE continuum.

NICE	BOLD	FIERCE

What's wrong here? Can't we all just get along?

It's not really that big a deal. I should just let it go. There's no need to make a fuss.

I was kind of hoping that it wouldn't come to this, but I guess I should speak up before it gets too late.

May I be totally honest with you?

Thanks for sharing your perspective. May I share mine with you now?

Let me start by telling you where I'm coming from on this, and then I want to hear from you.

I know it's going to hurt, but I don't know how else to tell this to you, and you really ought to know.

OK, I'm going to have to be brutally honest here with you.

Hey, I'm just saying what's true. If you can't handle it, that's your problem!

movement along the continuum, but not much. Most teams do not maintain the balance between the extremes. Occasionally a NICE team, for example, swings toward FIERCE in response to a crisis, but only temporarily. As soon as the crisis is over, members quickly revert to NICE. Correspondingly, a FIERCE team may shift to NICE briefly, perhaps in response to someone having read a book about the importance of teamwork. Once the novelty wears off, members return to FIERCE. Both kinds of teams would benefit by moving toward the center of the continuum.

There's no precisely "right" spot exactly in the middle. The ideal balance for some may not be right for others, but the goal is somewhere near the center.

What Does It Take to Be BOLD?

BOLD teams share components of NICE and FIERCE teams. The difference is that, rather than overemphasizing a single quality over another, as NICE and FIERCE teams do, they find balance.

BOLD teams find balance with compassion.

FIERCE teams know that they can't be their best by withholding truth. Members need information from each other to excel. BOLD teams know this, too, but, like NICE teams, they realize that the raw truth can do more harm than good.

For BOLD teams, then, the goal is not to protect one another from truth: It's to help each other by sharing vital information appropriately. To do that, BOLD teams deliver messages in a way that their teammates are able to hear. The truth doesn't have to hurt. BOLD team members have compassion for each other when they share their truth. They care about how the message is received, not just about getting the message across.

BOLD teams consider such things as which words to use, the tone of voice, body language, timing, setting, motives, and other factors. (More on these later in this chapter.) It takes effort to do this—effort that FIERCE teams neglect. The effort is borne of compassion that BOLD team members have for each other. Like NICE teams, they care a great deal about their relationships, but they use that compassion to share truth.

BOLD teams find balance with courage.

NICE teams know that strong team relationships are key to success. Teamwork happens when members work together. BOLD teams know this, too, but, like FIERCE teams, they accept that conflict occurs when people work together. So they don't shy away from confrontation.

BOLD teams bring together ideas, opinions, and perspectives for comparison. Inevitably they disagree on things. The goal, then, is not to prevent conflict, nor is it to win. The goal is to reach resolution. Toward that end, BOLD team members speak up—not just a few of them, all of them. They encourage each other to be heard.

Sometimes it takes courage to speak up and to stand alone on an issue. NICE teams muffle dissenters. FIERCE teams attack them. But BOLD teams welcome and respect different perspectives. The principle is not majority rules. It's hearing and respecting everyone's viewpoint, and then coming to a consensus that every BOLD team member can not just live with, but actually support wholeheartedly. Consensus can't happen if team members don't speak up with courage.

BOLD teams commit to balancing compassion and courage.

At one end of the continuum, NICE teams tend to be complacent. At the other end, FIERCE teams tend to be impersonal and aggressive. Moving from either end of the continuum toward BOLD takes effort and thus commitment. Staying BOLD requires team members to be vigilant in the short term, so that they can experience the payoff in the long term.

For NICE team members, keeping quiet is easy. If they do speak up, it takes little effort to make vague generalizations with no meat to them. BOLD requires people to speak up deliberately and specifically. NICE team members who want to be BOLD have to make the effort to be more open and straightforward. They must be committed to stretching and growing.

For FIERCE team members, saying whatever comes to mind in the moment, without censoring or editing, is easy. They just blurt it out and let the team deal with the effects of it. But BOLD requires people to be considerate of each other. FIERCE team members who want to be BOLD have to make the effort needed to check impulses and to consider the impact of their statements on others. They must be committed to stretching and growing.

BOLD teams commit to balancing compassion and courage. The work is hard, but they know that without compassion their team will slip into being FIERCE. Without courage, they will become NICE. Neither is acceptable. BOLD is the goal. BOLD is where the real payoff is, personally and collectively.

The Four BOLD Principles

Just trying to be more compassionate or courageous won't necessarily make a team BOLD. Putting out more effort is important, but only if it's the right kind of effort. How does a team become BOLD? The following four BOLD principles give you a framework for approaching nearly any situation where the truth needs to be shared in a respectful, caring way.

Principle 1: *Assume innocence.*

This is the most powerful principle for BOLD team members. The assumption of innocence comes from within and is at work before you even approach your teammate. Your attitude drives behavior, so it must be appropriately BOLD. Making assumptions about someone's underlying intentions is typical. It takes effort to withhold judgment and not jump to conclusions. It takes patience and trust to assume innocence, instead approaching others from a place of curiosity rather than accusation.

For example, Carmen is offended by something Scott did. "Why would he do that?" she asks. But she doesn't stop there. She provides her own answers by guessing at Scott's motives: "He's so lazy that he didn't do his planning. And then he thinks I'll jump in to help him with this project no matter what he needs or when." By assuming something other than Scott's innocence, she can get herself so worked up with suspicion or accusation that her next interaction with Scott cannot go well. If she's NICE, resentment and distrust will build as she whitewashes the trouble. Then she'll create work-arounds to avoid trouble in the future. If she's FIERCE, she'll blast Scott with her complaints.

BOLD team members don't go to either place because they assume innocence. Carmen wonders, "Why would he do that?" But then she suspends judgment until she gets the facts from Scott. She gives him the benefit of the doubt. She assumes that Scott did whatever he did because, from his perspective at the time, it was the most appropriate thing to do. He made the best possible choice given his circumstances. He was acting with good intentions, not just to cause Carmen more work or aggravation. She trusts this assumption.

Until she understands what truly motivated his action, she doesn't jump to conclusions or take any action. Rather than attacking him, getting revenge, ignoring him, or acquiescing resentfully, she takes a deep breath and assumes innocence. Then she plans to go directly to Scott to understand what happened.

Assuming innocence helps you build BOLD relationships with your teammates. Although there are three more BOLD principles, they are of little value if you don't first assume innocence. If you don't give your teammate the benefit of the doubt, then your contempt, distrust, anger, resentment, or whatever you're feeling will come through. You'll make accusations rather than ask questions. Even if you choose neutral words, it will still be clear that you are coming from a place of criticism, accusation, or mistrust—and *that* message will come through. Your tone of voice and body language will give your attitude away.

Here's the secret power of assuming innocence. Although the proven techniques in this book help teams reach BOLD authenticity with each other, you don't have to get them perfect (even you Perfectionists!). If you just start by assuming innocence, and if you come from a place of caring, the rest doesn't matter quite as much. Minor mistakes in technique, a few misspoken words, and a misstep here and there can be forgiven. What matters most is your intent. The techniques are important because they help you convey your intent effectively. But in the end, your true intent is more important than your technique.

Assume innocence before you even get started. Trust that, whatever people did or said, it made sense to them and was not intended to hurt or slight you.

Principle 2: *Build a bridge.*

Confrontations feel much more malicious to others when you just abruptly launch into them. There's no faster, easier way to make your teammates defensive than to jump on them without warning. That's not the goal of BOLD. The goal is resolution. Once you've gotten to the place of assuming innocence, the first step is to initiate a meaningful conversation with your teammate. Do that by building a bridge to invite your colleague to join you in dialogue.

The only way you can build a bridge is by knowing where the two ends of the bridge are. You know your position, but do you know the other so that you can build to it? If not, find out. If so, make sure. When teammates are talking, you should be listening—not planning your rebuttal or looking for ammo for your retort. Use active listening skills to be sure you understand: ask questions for clarification and paraphrase what you think you hear. You can't build a bridge to nowhere; you must know their position before you can proceed with any purpose.

Stephen R. Covey says it quite simply: "Seek first to understand."

For Carmen, this requirement may mean asking Scott for more information about his actions.

> Please tell me more about how you came to that decision, Scott.

Because she's the one initiating the conversation, it's her responsibility to seek to understand Scott first. Then she can build a bridge and begin collaboration and resolution. Scott is more apt to hear Carmen's position after he's convinced she's heard his.

Once she understands him, Carmen can introduce her concern in a way that helps Scott see *beyond* his own perspective. She's ready to build that bridge, and she does so with empathy and understanding.

> It sounds like you prefer to see the project unfold step by step so that you can be sure the quality is high. It's difficult to track everything that's going on with a project this big.

And I'm with you on the quality. I want it high, too! So it makes sense to me that you would need my help right now at this step. May I share my perspective on how this has affected me?

Notice how she doesn't give Scott a generic, "Yes, project management is challenging, but . . . ." She specifically acknowledges his efforts on the project and does so personally. She obviously understands how he is approaching this project and even why. Her empathy is the bridge that will take him from his position to at least hearing hers. She took all these steps because she came to him from a place of caring. She assumed his innocence before she ever spoke a word.

Of course, building a bridge may be as simple as just checking to make sure your teammate is ready to hear your truth.

Scott, may I give you some feedback about how this project is affecting me?

Now if Scott just got chewed out by the boss or if personal issues or other things are going on, he may not be in a state of mind to hear Carmen, much less have a dialogue with her. So it's important to ask—in a respectful way—if this is a good time to talk before you launch into clearing the air.

FIERCE teams ignore this principle. Team members just jump into confrontation without warning. If anything, they build walls rather than bridges. They gear up for the confrontation by fortifying their positions or by bringing in allies before the fireworks begin.

NICE teams get stuck at this point. They build a bridge

and then congratulate themselves for having built it, but they don't use it. Instead, they admire the bridge. They talk about strengthening it and adding to it. Their focus shifts from the point of contention to the bridge itself: "See how great this bridge is that we built? We work together so well! I bet we could make it even better if we added lampposts and potted plants. How about a public bench?"

There is one word to avoid in building a bridge: *but*. *But* means, "Please disregard everything you've heard up to this point because I'm about to tell you the honest truth now." Watch how *but* works:

> It sounds like you prefer to see the project unfold step by step so that you can be sure the quality is high. It's difficult to track everything that's going on with a project this big. And I'm with you on the quality. I want it high, too! So it makes sense to me that you would need my help right now at this step, *but* your approach has affected me too. May I share my perspective?

The *but* negates all the compassion Carmen showed earlier. It suggests that the impact on her is more important than what Scott is experiencing.

The easiest way around using *but* is to use *and* instead. Grammatically, it always works. Hear the difference in Carmen's comments:

> It sounds like you prefer to see the project unfold step by step so that you can be sure the quality is high. It's difficult to track everything that's going on with a project this big. And I'm with you on the quality. I want it high, too! So it makes sense to me that you would need my help right now

at this step, *and* your approach has affected me too. May I share my perspective?

Note the difference the *and* makes on the way the message comes across. The *but* discounted everything Carmen said up to that word. The *and* joins what she said about her understanding of Scott's experience with her next comments.

Even worse than bridging your comments with a *but* is to start them off with it.

> *But* the way you're managing this project is affecting me, too. May I share my perspective?

The first word—*but*—is Carmen's entrée. It's not a bridge; it's a wall. You can almost see her putting her hand in front of Scott's face as she stops him cold and proceeds to state her position. Just changing the *but* to an *and* makes a big difference in how she comes across. It's not the best bridge in the world, but *and* is far better than beginning with a *but*.

Initiate the conversation by building a bridge. Respect your team members enough to prepare them to hear your truth, and do so only when they are ready.

Principle 3: *Speak your truth.*

Notice the word *your*. There is no absolute truth in human interactions. Carmen has hers; Scott has his. She believes that what happened from her perspective is truth. And Scott believes his experience is truth. They each have different truths.

The essence of authenticity is speaking your own truth so

that others can hear and understand it. From that understanding comes resolution that's meaningful and beneficial to all parties involved.

This is where courage comes into play. You can't speak your truth without courage. It takes guts to look someone in the eye and say something that he or she will disagree with or that you know they don't want to hear. The courage you need comes from caring about your teammates and your relationships with them. It comes from trusting that what you have to say will actually make a difference—for them, for you, for the team, or for the work.

The secret to speaking your truth is to be objective. Vague language doesn't help: The more specific you can be, the better the resolution will be. Objectivity may be more difficult than it seems. When Carmen says, "Scott, you didn't plan very well," she is giving him feedback. Unfortunately, it is so vague that it's not terribly helpful. It puts him on notice that she's not pleased and he may get hurt or defensive, but that's about it. She needs to be more specific and objective.

> Scott, you didn't complete a project plan. You took each task one at a time when you could have accomplished several things at once. You never shared with me what you were going to need or expect from me. Each time you've needed my input, you've asked for it that very day.

Notice the absence of judgment or criticism. She's merely stating the facts as she knows them. She's sharing her truth.

She's not finished, though, until she shares the rest of her truth: the impact. Scott's actions are one thing. How they affected Carmen is another.

> Scott, you didn't complete a project plan. You took each task one at a time when you could have accomplished several things at once. Because of that, you didn't share what you were going to need or expect from me and when. Each time you've needed my input, you've asked for it that very day. Without a project plan, I couldn't prepare in advance to give you what you needed, when you needed it. When you came to me with same-day requests, sometimes I wasn't able to respond. That delayed (and frustrated) you. Other times, I was able to just give a gut reaction without any serious analysis. I felt like I couldn't give you my best work. I even began to wonder how much you really wanted or valued my input when you kept asking for it when you did.

Here again, there is no judgment or criticism. At the end she said "asking for it when you did." She could have said "asking for it as late as you did" or "asking for it at the last minute." But she continues to assume innocence in his timing of requests and keeps her message as neutral as possible.

Stating your truth about something is very helpful. Describing its impact on you, on others, or on the work makes your statement even more compelling. FIERCE teams tend to speak as if truth is absolute. Arguments erupt over who is "right" or whose perspective is accurate. NICE teams conform to each other's truth so readily that individual truth doesn't get its due consideration.

Speak your truth. Tell it like it is without embellishment, and then share its impact as accurately and as fairly as you can.

Principle 4: *Invite dialogue.*

So you have assumed innocence. You have led off by building a bridge for understanding. Then you have shared your
truth. You're not done yet. You have one more thing to do:
True resolution doesn't happen until there's a dialogue about
what you said. Your truth is important, and so is your teammate's. Invite him or her to share it with you.

Warning: This invitation takes every bit as much courage
as speaking your truth does!

Carmen could say simply, "So, Scott, how do you see
this?" or "I'm anxious to hear your perspective, Scott." As
Scott speaks his own truth, Carmen's job is to listen and hear
what he has to say, always assuming innocence.

Team members who haven't read this book may respond
from a place of hurt, defensiveness, or even aggression. Hear
them out, don't take things personally, and stay in your place
of curiosity (i.e., keep assuming innocence). Ask questions to
clarify their reactions and help them speak their truth in more
specific and objective terms.

Only when you hear your teammate's truth can you have
a meaningful conversation and true dialogue about the issue,
eventually reaching an efficient, effective, and lasting resolution. A NICE team doesn't get there because the members
back off as soon as they share their truth. A FIERCE team
doesn't get there because the members insist on being understood first. And once they are understood, they assume others
will naturally agree with them (not likely). A BOLD team
encourages curiosity and understanding, not abandonment or
insistence.

Invite dialogue. Let curiosity replace assumptions and accusations.

Figure 4–3 shows how the BOLD principles compare to the more common NICE and FIERCE ones.

Figure 4-3. NICE-BOLD-FIERCE norms.

Step	NICE	BOLD	FIERCE
1.	Assume malice— they're acting in their own best interest—and then create work-arounds.	Assume innocence—they're acting in what they believed were everyone's best interests—and then approach from a place of trust, caring, and curiosity	Assume malice— they're acting in their own best interests— and then react quickly and sharply.
2.	Build multiple, duplicate bridges; excessive bridge building looks like collaboration, and it's a great way to avoid confrontation.	Build a bridge. Understand their perspective first, and then use that understanding to introduce your perspective in a way that they can hear and appreciate.	Skip the bridges. Their perspective isn't as important as yours, and it may be worthwhile to build some walls just in case it gets ugly later.
3.	Speak what may be *a* truth, and then back off quickly if it's questioned, challenged, or even ignored at first.	Speak your truth. Share your perspective objectively and specifically (honesty without brutality). Then follow up with your rationale so that teammates appreciate your motives.	Speak *the* truth. There's only one real truth: yours. Stick to your guns, and don't give in until they see things your way.
4.	Smooth things over. Apologize, backtrack, and soften the message each time you repeat it until eventually everyone feels better.	Invite dialogue. Actively seek response or reaction to your truth. Listen carefully to the other team member's truth (assuming innocence) and seek to fully understand it before moving to resolution together.	Demand understanding. Insist that others truly hear and understand you first. It will help them agree with you all the more quickly and completely.

The next three chapters will show you specifically how to put these principles into action in three types of team interactions:

◘ Chapter 5 will lay out the steps for giving feedback.

- Chapter 6 will describe a process for making requests of teammates.

- Chapter 7 will show you how to disagree with teammates appropriately.

Tips for Confronting Others Using BOLD Principles

Being BOLD is about managing and leveraging confrontation effectively. The goal of confronting someone is resolution, not winning, gaining power, or belittling people. Apply the following tips to the BOLD principles to help teammates avoid reactions that are defensive, pessimistic, or otherwise counterproductive. If you have assumed innocence and are truly coming from a place of caring, these tips will help you convey that.

- *Use a person's name, and use it often.* There's no better way to keep the interaction personal than to use your teammate's name. It's difficult to make oversimplifications or grand generalizations when you are talking to a Carmen or a Scott, instead of "you" or "you people." People tend to soften at the sound of their name, as long as it's used respectfully. Avoid overdoing this, though, so that you don't sound phony.

- *Give them your full, undivided attention, including eye contact.* Look them in the eye so that they can see your real intent. People tend to trust others who look them in the eye. BOLD is about being authentic. Eye contact is important for helping others believe that what you are saying is your truth and that you are saying it to help them or the team.

◻ *Watch your tone of voice.* How many times have you been told, "It's not *what* you said, but *how* you said it!" Your tone shows more about your intent and your attitude than the words you choose. Be careful that you are not delivering your message with a raised voice, a condescending tone, monotone, or in any other way that contradicts your true intent. The easiest way to do this is to assume innocence.

◻ *Watch your body language.* People trust what they see more than what they hear in your words. For this reason, BOLD conversations are always best done face to face. If you lean too far forward, you may be perceived as being aggressive. Sit back too casually, and you may be perceived as not taking the conversation seriously or as condescending. A comfortable posture is best. Genuine gestures, perhaps toned down just a bit, are good.

◻ *Don't beat around the bush.* Talking around the issue is not helpful: it's confusing and distracting. Once you're ready to say your truth, just say it. Most people prefer being told something directly rather than trying to guess what you mean. Be direct, straightforward, and to the point.

◻ *Avoid blaming others.* When delivering a difficult message, don't blame anyone for making you deliver it. While others' actions may have put you into the situation, calling that out doesn't add to your relationship with your teammate. It usually lessens his or her opinion of you and makes the message seem less sincere.

❏ *Give empathy where appropriate.* Empathy is merely acknowledging what the other person is experiencing. It doesn't mean you agree with the feeling. Nor does it mean you have to apologize. Just acknowledge that you recognize what the person is going through. Don't tell them that you "know how they feel." You don't. You may be able to piece together an understanding, but unless you've had the very same life experiences they have, you can't *know* how they feel. Be careful not to incite them with this empty phrase of empathy.

❏ *Allow them their reactions.* Reactions may include crying, anger, frustration, irritation, annoyance, blaming, defensiveness, and a whole lot more. Empathy includes allowing your teammates to feel or experience whatever reactions they have. It's not your place to tell them how to feel, even if you have good intentions: "Scott, you shouldn't feel frustrated about this." Scott may feel however he feels, including frustrated. Telling people not to feel something doesn't prevent them from feeling it. Use empathy only to acknowledge their emotional experience. Don't try to fix it: "Scott, I can see how frustrated you are about this." Emotional reactions are all too human. Allow them their humanity, and honor it.

Suggestions for Each of the Nine NICE Team Players as They Use the BOLD Principles

The NICE team players all face personal challenges to working in a BOLD environment. Here are points for them to remember:

- *Peacemakers.* Bring focus to the issues and don't get sidetracked with interesting, although not critical, tangents.

- *Champions.* Remember that "feeling screwed" is not the same as "being screwed." Check your impulses and assume innocence.

- *Perfectionists.* Accept that it's perfectly human to have imperfections, and remember that perfect intent is more important than perfect execution.

- *Energizers.* Be patient and explore the depths of issues with others, even though that means having difficult conversations at times.

- *Guardians.* Let go of worry and suspicion, and trust your inner authority.

- *Observers.* Accept feelings as a unique source of information about the world around you, and balance observation with participation.

- *Individualists.* Commit yourself to stable standards and clear principles to guide you through the ups and downs of conflict resolution.

◻ *Achievers*. Look beyond self-interest to the common good of the team, and watch your tendency to embellish or put a spin on your truth.

◻ *Helpers*. Balance others' needs with your own, and remember that the rest of us are not "defective Helpers"; we'll never anticipate your needs as well as you do ours. So it's OK to speak up about your own needs.

Summary

◻ NICE and FIERCE are at two ends of a spectrum, where NICE emphasizes protecting people from hurt and FIERCE emphasizes asserting truth. In the middle is BOLD, which values asserting truth, but with consideration for people.

◻ BOLD teams succeed by balancing courage (speaking truth) with compassion (speaking that truth respectfully and considerately). They accept that this balancing act requires a real commitment of effort.

◻ There are four BOLD Principles:

1. *Assume innocence*. Come from a place of caring and trust before launching into a BOLD conversation. Plan the timing and setting for difficult discussions. Do this before you approach your teammate.

2. *Build a bridge*. Begin by making sure your teammate is ready to have a conversation with you. Lay the groundwork so that you can link your teammate's position with what you have to say.

3. *Speak your truth.* Be objective and specific. Then share the relevance of your comments to your teammate's reality.

4. *Invite dialogue.* Ask your teammates to share their perspectives. Be prepared for their disagreement or pushback. Respond in a way that helps move you and your teammates toward true resolution.

▫ When having a BOLD conversation, keep these things in mind:

- Use a person's name, and use it often.
- Give others your full, undivided attention, including eye contact.
- Watch your tone of voice.
- Watch your body language.
- Don't beat around the bush.
- Avoid blaming others.
- Give empathy where appropriate.
- Allow others their reactions.

▫ Know what type of team member you are, and watch for the characteristics that may block you from being BOLD.

◆ ◆ ◆

Whenever you're in conflict with someone, there is one factor that can make the difference between damaging your relationship and deepening it. That factor is attitude.

WILLIAM JAMES

5

BOLD Feedback

Sticks and stones may break my bones, but words will make me go in a corner and cry by myself for hours.

ERIC IDLE

To give feedback is to share your perspective about the past. It's to give information to your teammates that they may not have. Here's what it's *not:*

◻ *Hindsight.* Telling people what they should have done.
◻ *Criticism.* Telling them that what they did was good or bad.
◻ *Direction.* Telling them what they should do.

BOLD feedback is merely telling them how you experienced their actions—plain and simple.

Feedback is a critical cornerstone of BOLD teams. People need feedback to improve; they can't develop without it. The team won't progress if its members don't give each other feedback that helps them get better—individually and together. Friction in a team arises from innocent actions that get ignored or worked around. *Feedback is the primary mechanism for addressing behaviors that would otherwise hold people back.*

BOLD feedback requires an appropriate balance of compassion and courage. And BOLD team members must be committed to the effort it takes to deliver feedback well. Without compassion, feedback comes across as faultfinding and judgmental. Without courage, it either comes across as whining and complaining, or it gets so whitewashed that it loses all meaning.

By using the four principles of BOLD, you can deliver feedback that your teammates will hear and act on, while you minimize their resentment or defensiveness.

Principle 1. Assume innocence.

Step 1: *Make your feedback sincere.*

Why are you offering feedback? If you aren't doing it from a place of caring—truly wanting to promote your teammates' development—it comes across as criticism and invites defensiveness on their part. People can sense your motives, no matter which words you choose. Your tone of voice and your body language betray you if your motive is anything short of sincere helpfulness.

When you care, your feedback to them comes across

more sincerely. You are more apt to use their names naturally and make comments that communicate personally. Your message is less likely to come across as stilted or rehearsed.

Before you approach giving feedback, make sure you are not feeling frustrated, angry, resentful, vengeful, critical, or wanting to find fault. Your motive must come from your heart. If you're not there yet, wait to give feedback until you are.

Sometimes it is your job to give feedback. You may be the boss or a quality expert. If that's the only reason you are offering feedback, your voice and body language project feeling. The people you're speaking with are much less apt to accept your obligatory feedback as anything more than just that. Get yourself into a position of caring about a person's improvement before offering feedback.

It doesn't matter how well you word the feedback. It doesn't matter how well you prepare for it. It doesn't matter how professionally you give it. It doesn't matter which feedback model you use. If your heart is not in it, your voice and body language communicate the lack of sincerity, whether you realize it or not. Remember: Your intent is more important than your technique. That said, you can use the techniques in this book to help you be more effective, but they work only when you actually care.

Step 2: *Make your feedback timely.*

When is it best to give feedback? Do it as soon as possible after the behavior or impact in question, when your teammates can still remember the details of what they did and even why. They can also remember the moment or the situation well enough to connect their behavior with what you tell them.

Consider the following examples. Which is more likely to influence Jada's behavior?

> Jada, may I give you some feedback about that presentation you did this morning?

> Jada, I've been meaning to give you feedback about that presentation you did a few months ago. May I do that now?

Although you want to choose a time that is as close to the behavior as possible, be sensitive to your teammate's frame of mind. For example, launching into an in-depth analysis of Jada's presentation the moment she takes her seat may be too soon, even if she leans over and whispers, "How did I do?" At that point, just give a quick assessment and then offer to give more details (and more help) later. "You did great. Good energy! Let's talk more later, OK?"

If you wait too long, however, your teammate may forget things that would be helpful for improvement. Waiting too long also invites resentment: "Why didn't you tell me this before? Why did you wait until now to bring this up?"

Use your best judgment to determine your timing. If your approach is caring, you'll know when the best time is.

Step 3: *Choose a comfortable place.*

Give feedback in an environment that makes your teammate (not you) the most comfortable. Eliminate anything that may prevent someone from hearing what you have to say. Avoid locations that are noisy, have too many visual distractions, are within earshot of others, are visible to others (enclosed offices with glass walls), are too hot or too cold, are places where you're likely to be interrupted, or may be intimidating (e.g., sitting behind your desk can be intimidating to some).

If the feedback is not *positive, deliver it in private.* No one wants to be embarrassed in front of others, no matter how much you think others could benefit from what you have to say. Deliver the feedback in private and then paraphrase any learning for others later, if necessary. Stay away from connecting your comments with any one individual.

If the feedback is positive, consider the receiver before automatically delivering it in public. Some people prefer not to be called out in public. They find it embarrassing. They may perceive your positive feedback as negative if it is delivered in a public setting.

Don't be afraid to ask your teammate to follow you to an appropriate location before delivering your feedback. Remember: this is an important piece of information you are about to share. Take a moment to be sure they are ready to hear it—even if that requires you to walk to a more appropriate place. If you care about this person, tending to the environment should not be a nuisance.

Principle 2. Build a bridge.

Step 4: *Preface your request with feedback.*

Are our teammates ready to hear you? If not, it doesn't matter how valuable your feedback is or how eloquently you

deliver it. You won't be able to help them if they aren't ready
for your help. Ideally, they'll ask for your feedback. But if
they don't, asking permission to share your feedback with
them is the next best thing.

> Jada, I'd like to give you some feedback on your presentation
> yesterday afternoon. Would that be OK with you?

Rarely does someone refuse. Just the act of asking shows
respect. Without being asked, however, your teammates may
resent your pressing your opinion on them uninvited. They
may see you as being overbearing. Sure, you may need to get
something off your chest, but whose needs are you meeting
then? Ask first. If someone refuses, check your motivation
again before insisting on pressing forward for the sake of
"being authentic."

You may be required to give feedback regardless of anyone's willingness to receive it. Perhaps you're the boss. As
such, it's your job to give feedback and adjust behavior. If so,
team members don't have an option to refuse your feedback.
They may not want to hear it, but they are going to anyway,
right? You can still demonstrate respect. Rather than asking
permission to share feedback, ask *when* they want to hear it.

> Jada, I'd like to give you some feedback on your presentation
> this morning. Which works better for you: doing that now
> or after our staff meeting tomorrow?

If you're Jada's boss, giving her some choice about *when*
she hears your feedback, instead of *whether* she hears it, recog-

nizes your right to impose feedback. But it also respects her as an adult by allowing her to have a say about timing.

Principle 3. Speak your truth.

Step 5: *Be specific and objective.*

What happened? What did you hear or see—or not hear or see? Tell your teammate what specific behavior or action or results you or others witnessed. Remain objective. Do this to avoid arguments about any interpretation of the facts. Arguments over interpretation take you both off the real issue and into a no-win situation. Either your teammate did or they did not do what you say happened. No one has to argue about why, nor about what it means.

Stick to the facts and your teammates are much less likely to refute the feedback.

Which of these examples is less apt to provoke a defensive, argumentative response?

Jada, you weren't very prepared for your presentation.

Jada, in your presentation, you looked at your notes a lot. In fact, three times you read straight from your notes for more than a minute or two.

Don't interpret or label her behavior. Stick to the facts: Jada read from her notes three times. She will give very little pushback on such feedback. It happened. She was there. We were all watching. The danger comes when the behavior is labeled.

> Jada, in your presentation, you looked at your notes a lot. In
> fact, three times you read straight from your notes for more
> than a minute or two. Obviously you didn't prepare very
> well for this presentation.

How do you know she didn't prepare? Maybe she prepared for hours but wasn't very organized in her preparation.
Maybe she prepared, but just didn't care enough to try very
hard. Maybe she had a negative attitude about the presentation. Maybe a personal issue was distracting her. Maybe she
was nervous about speaking in front of groups. Thankfully,
you don't have to make that call—so don't! Just give her
BOLD feedback so that she can find ways not to read from
her notes again.

Without the interpretation, your conversation is simpler
and more productive. With it, however, you invite Jada to
disagree with you. Quickly the discussion can deteriorate
into an argument over whether she was prepared. Being prepared isn't the issue; reading from her notes is. Keep the focus
on her behavior and away from your interpretation of it.
Later, she may admit to not preparing well, but let her say it.
BOLD feedback is not about being right or catching her, it's
about helping her be successful (because you care).

Clarify vague terms with behavioral specifics. Being specific
helps your teammates clearly understand exactly what you
mean. Avoid using vague terms or labels: *bad attitude, low
initiative, uncooperative, poor leadership skills, negative attitude, not
a team player, difficult to work with, poor communicator.* Positive-
sounding labels are just as unhelpful: *dedicated, helpful, good*

customer service skills, great leader, dependable, supportive, good attitude, and the like.

Being specific with feedback particularly means that there is no place for commenting on teammates' attitude, even if you think they have a bad one. *Attitude* is not a specific enough word to help anyone improve.

Consider this example. What should Brett do after hearing this?

> Brett, when you first joined the team, you were very enthused. Lately I've noticed your attitude isn't as good. I hope you don't take this wrong, but I just want you to have a good attitude about the work like the rest of us, OK?

Brett would be hard-pressed to figure out how to improve his attitude.

So how do you give feedback if all you have to say is that Brett has a bad attitude? You start by assuming innocence—that he doesn't have a bad attitude or that, if he does, he has a valid reason for it. It's not up to you to discover the reason. Your job is actually much easier. Coming from a place of caring about Brett, you want to give feedback that will help him improve how he comes across. "You have a bad attitude" doesn't help him. So, as you plan your conversation with him, ask yourself how you know that Brett has a bad attitude. What evidence do you have? Keep asking until your answers focus on specific behaviors.

> Brett has a bad attitude.
>   How do I know this? He doesn't seem to care.

And how do I know this? He just doesn't seem to want to be part of the team.

What evidence do I have of this? Well, he never seems to demonstrate initiative.

What do I mean by initiative? When there are no customers in the store, he just stands around and waits for the next one. He never cleans or restocks anything.

Finally, you have some feedback that Brett can use. Notice that each of the responses before that was just a different, equally vague generalization about Brett's behavior.

Look at these examples. Which would be most effective in helping Brett with his attitude?

Brett, I don't think your attitude is so great these days.

Brett, when the store is empty, you stand around and wait for more customers. You don't clean anything or stock anything. This makes it harder for everyone else to keep the store clean and stocked for when we do have a rush of customers.

Tie your feedback to specifics. This helps Brett focus on what's real. Generalizations and labels encourage him to be defensive, or to dismiss the feedback when he can't figure out what the real issue is.

Another way to generalize is to use absolutes—*always, never, constantly,* and so on. Going back to Jada, how might she react to these statements?

Jada, you always read from your notes when you make presentations. Notes are just supposed to help you, not be a crutch for a lack of preparation.

You sure like your notes. You read from them constantly throughout your presentation. You wouldn't need them all the time if you prepared better.

You're never prepared for your presentations, Jada. You always need too many notes, and you use them as a crutch.

All three of these examples use generalizations that would inflame Jada. The absolutes generalize her behavior rather than pinpoint it. Absolutes are never accurate. (Yes, *that* absolute statement is on purpose!) Don't give your teammates reasons to be defensive. Don't give them anything to distract from the pure feedback of what you observed.

Don't comment on what should have happened. Don't comment on what should happen in the future, either. Stick to what *did* happen. BOLD feedback is always spoken in the past tense: what was. It's an observation of a prior event. But if you do only that, how can you really help your teammate? Shouldn't you say what to do? You see the solution so clearly; shouldn't you share it with your teammates?

Solving the problem may help in the short term, but it usually doesn't help in the long run. It may make you feel smart, but it does little to build your teammates' problem-solving skills or their confidence. Remember why you are giving feedback. Curb your enthusiasm to do it for them. Check your ego. Offer BOLD feedback, and let them find their own solution (perhaps with your help). Offering solutions at this point limits your teammates' options.

In this example, how many options does Jada have for improving her presentation next time?

So next time you make a presentation, Jada, I think you should write down only the main points on your cards, not the full text. That will force you to look at the audience and not read to them.

Jada has two options. Do as suggested or not. If she does what is suggested and her next presentation goes poorly, who's responsible? *You* are. You're the one who solved her note-reading problem for her. If she fails, you obviously gave her a poor solution. And what did Jada learn in the process?

When you don't offer options in your feedback to Jada, how many options does she have for improving her presentation?

I'm curious about what caused you to rely so heavily on your notes, Jada. That may give you ideas for what to do next time . . .

I wonder what you could do, Jada, so that the notes get less emphasis in your next presentation.

After commenting on what you observed, remain silent. Let Jada fill the silence with her thoughts about how she may improve. Consider how many options are available to Jada with comments like these. She can memorize her presentation. She can put an outline on her cards rather than the entire text. She can get a copresenter to help her. She can put part of her presentation into a prerecorded video. She can add more charts and graphs to depict some points. The options are limitless. Who's responsibility is it for her to be successful next time? Hers. And if she is still unsuccessful, who's problem is it? Still hers, not yours. And if she is successful? Hooray! Celebrate with her.

If you feel a strong need to tell a teammate how to improve, follow the steps in Chapter 6 for making such requests or recommendations.

Step 6: *Make it relevant to the organization.*

Why does the feedback matter? What impact did your teammate's actions have on you, your clients, other teammates, sales, internal processes, timelines, projects, or anything else that is important? If you can't point to how your teammate's actions or results affected the organization, you probably shouldn't be giving the feedback. Show the impact, preferably with irrefutable facts and figures. This way, you avoid arguments about the validity of your assessment.

In this example, which comments are more likely to convince Jada to change the way she presents in the future?

> Jada, in your presentation, you looked at your notes a lot. In fact, three times you read straight from your notes for more than a minute or two.

> Jada, in your presentation, you looked at your notes a lot. In fact, three times you read straight from your notes for more than a minute or two. When you did this, you weren't able to make eye contact with your audience. I saw several people raise their hands with questions, and then put them back down. I'm concerned that they didn't get the clarity they needed to understand our team's message.

After hearing the first example, Jada may or may not understand the seriousness of reading from her notes. After the second example, it's very clear.

There's no need to add emphasis or drama to your explanation of the impact. Your teammate easily sees through this tactic, and it discredits the validity of your feedback, rather than strengthening it.

Compare the following approach with the last one. Which is Jada more likely to hear?

> Jada, in your presentation, you looked at your notes a lot. In fact, three times you read straight from your notes for more than a minute or two. When you did this, you couldn't make eye contact, and you missed a bunch of questions the group probably had. Lots of people raised their hands and then put them back down. They had critical questions that others shared. Now we don't know who knows what, and we'll have to redo this whole presentation to make sure everyone gets it. People will be frustrated that they have to sit through it again—all because you read your notes and didn't pay attention to your audience.

The preceding example is so inflated that Jada is likely to reject the entire message, including the valid feedback. The one before it is accurate and gives Jada the information she needs to improve her presentation skills.

Principle 4. Invite dialogue.

Step 7: *Make this a discussion.*

After you deliver feedback, your teammate will respond. What kind of reaction do you expect? Anger? Blaming? Hurt? Confusion? Silence? Defensiveness? Deflecting? Avoidance? The better you know your teammates (and the more often you give them feedback), the better you are able to predict their responses and prepare for them.

After you've shared your feedback, invite a response or reaction—as scary as doing so may seem! If the reaction is emotional, the teammate needs to work through it before being ready to accept your gift of feedback. Your efforts so far will be wasted if you don't help your teammate get through the emotion. Listen without getting defensive. People usually just want to justify what they did. You've assumed innocence, so now they can fill you in on their experience at the time. After you've heard the reaction, first be empathetic. Acknowledge the feelings. You don't have to agree. You don't have to apologize. Just acknowledge that you heard your colleague and that you "get" where he or she is coming from.

> Wow, Jada, it sounds like this is pretty upsetting to you. You put a lot of effort into your presentation and so it's disappointing that you didn't come across as well as you had hoped.

Paraphrase what she said, and acknowledge how she feels. *Then* go on to respond to her comments and discuss the issue at hand.

Anticipate your teammate's reaction so that you are ready to deal with it. Although the most common reactions are defensiveness, anger, and blaming others, your teammate may respond differently. Play it out in your mind. Imagine the team member crying or clamming up. Explore different ways you may respond to work through any negative reaction and get refocused on your helpful message.

When information is shared, misunderstandings and skewed perceptions are cleared up—and not just someone else's. Be open to having your own sense of reality altered as you get new information from them.

Step 8: *Make the discussion a start, not an end.*

What are the next steps for both of you? Although your colleague has the primary responsibility to make fixes, it's also his or her choice. It's not your job to force a fix—unless you're the boss.

If you have ideas on how to improve, now is the time to offer them. Ideally, your teammate asks for your advice, but, if not, go ahead and offer. Chapter 6 will show you how to make suggestions at this point, at the same time strengthening your relationship.

Whether someone wants your input or not, at least offer your support in resolving the situation. At a minimum, you can pledge to give interim feedback as the teammate works on changing or improving.

Lastly, offer a word of genuine encouragement. This should be easy regardless of the reaction, as long as you've approached the interaction in caring way.

Positive Feedback

Be just as rigorous giving positive feedback as you are with the constructive or developmental kind. Pay particular attention to ensuring that your positive feedback is specific, objective, and relevant to the organization.

Consider the following examples. Which would encourage Sara to repeat her actions?

Great job on the report, Sara. Keep up the good work!

Great job on the report, Sara. I especially like the way you organized the sales figures by state as well as by region. The columns you created to distinguish between the two made it so much easier for me to see where our strengths are. I was also able to quickly see where we need to better leverage our sales force.

After hearing the first comment, Sara may go away thinking that getting the entire report onto a single page was the key, or was it omitting the footnotes that used to clutter up the report? In the future, that may be her focus. The second example leaves no room for misunderstanding what she did so well—and what would be appreciated next time.

Feedback is simply information you share about your perspective on something from the past: your experience. Offer it from a place of caring, or don't offer it at all.

Use the worksheet in Appendix 4 to outline how to give feedback to a teammate.

Summary

◻ Feedback is telling people how you experienced their actions, without criticizing, fixing, judging, or directing them. Removing the pressure to judge or fix teammates frees you up to truly *help* each other.

◻ The eight steps of BOLD feedback coincide with the four BOLD strategies:

- Step 1: Make your feedback sincere. *(Assume innocence.)* Why are you offering feedback?
- Step 2: Make your feedback timely. When will you give the feedback?
- Step 3: Choose a comfortable environment. Where will you give the feedback?
- Step 4: Make it OK to give feedback. *(Build a bridge.)* Is the person ready to hear you?
- Step 5: Make it specific and objective. *(Share your truth.)* What happened?
- Step 6: Make it relevant to the organization. Why does this feedback matter?
- Step 7: Make this a discussion. *(Invite dialogue.)* What kind of reaction do you expect?
- Step 8: Make the discussion a start, not an end. What are the next steps for both of you?

◻ Be just as rigorous giving positive feedback as giving the constructive or developmental kind. Follow the steps, and be just as specific and objective.

♦ ♦ ♦

One of the chief misfortunes of honest people is that they are cowardly.

Voltaire

6

BOLD Requests

Don't pretend that it's OK. Things won't get better that way.

SHANIA TWAIN

To make a request is to ask for something you want or need. It's about taking care of yourself *and* making sure that your relationship with your teammate is working for both of you. It's not about staying quiet regarding your needs or suffering for the good of the team. That's NICE. It's not about demanding that all other team members adjust their style to meet your needs, either. That's FIERCE. It's about speaking up when something's getting in the way of your doing your best for the team and then seeking a different approach.

Requests are critical on BOLD teams. People are not mindreaders. They often don't know what you want or need from them unless you tell them. It's nothing personal. They interact with you the way they've learned is best for them. But you are unique, so how they work with others may not be good with you. That's when you need to speak up and help them. When team members aren't specific about their needs or expectations, disappointment and resentment build quickly on the team.

BOLD requests, like anything else BOLD, require compassion and courage. Without compassion, requests come across as demands or ultimatums. Without courage, requests come across as begging or as not important enough to be taken seriously.

When you speak up about what you need, little problems can be resolved before they fester and grow. The sooner you speak up, the easier it is to prevent or fix a problem. The sooner you speak up, the easier it is for your teammate to hear you and to adjust.

Here is a step-by-step approach to making BOLD requests, using the four BOLD principles identified in Chapter 4.

Assume Innocence

Step 1: *Approach others with respect.*

Why should your teammates change? Obviously they do what they do because it makes sense to them. No one wakes up in the morning and thinks, "Hmm, how can I make life miserable for others?" Whatever it is that you would like to change, people don't do it because they are mean, vindictive, or vengeful, but because it seems logical to them. It benefits them somehow or at least it doesn't hurt them. They may not even be aware of its impact on you.

Assume your teammates are acting out of innocence or at least without malice. Otherwise, you come across as critical, demanding, or possibly arrogant. Teammates then figure that your motive is to "fix" them, settle a score, or avenge some alleged wrongdoing. They shut down and not hear you, or they hear you and defensively reject your request. Approach them with respect, and they are at least open to hearing your request. They may not agree to it, but they are more likely to listen with an open mind and want to find a resolution together.

So before you make a request, be sure you are not coming from a place of suspicion, condescension, accusation, anger, or revenge. Your motives must be genuine and without guile. If you're not there yet, hold your request until you are.

Step 2: *Choose a good time.*

When will you make your request? NICE team players tend to wait. And wait. "Maybe my teammate will change. Maybe I'll get used to this, and it won't get in the way anymore. Maybe she'll see how her actions are affecting others. Maybe he'll come around naturally. All they need is a little more time." Meanwhile, your resentment builds and nothing gets better for anyone.

Waiting also makes it more difficult to request something, and the request grows bigger with each passing day.

In the following examples, which request sounds and feels bigger—and harder—to make?

> Luis, I've noticed something the last couple of times we've met that is starting to get in the way for me, and I was hoping we could talk about it.

> Luis, over the years, every time we meet, something has gotten in the way for me, and I think it's probably time we talk about it.

In the second example, Luis is going to be defensive. He will assume that years of buildup have created something pretty big. And if it's big, he better prepare to defend whatever it was he has been doing all this time.

On the other hand, you shouldn't make a request the moment one enters your mind. Take some time to reflect on it. Make sure that it warrants yours and your teammate's energy before you bring it up.

Step 3: *Choose a comfortable environment.*

Where will you make your request? As in the case of giving feedback, submit your request in a place that makes your teammate (not necessarily you) the most comfortable. Eliminate anything that may get in the way of your teammate's hearing what you have to say. Avoid locations that are noisy, have too many visual distractions, are within earshot of others, are visible to others (enclosed offices with glass walls), are too hot or too cold, invite interruption, or seem intimidating (such as you sitting behind your desk).

Make your request in private. Your teammate will feel

less put on the spot and will be more likely to engage in an honest discussion there, too.

> This is an important change you are about to request. Take a moment to be sure that your teammate is ready to hear it, even if that requires you to move to a more appropriate place.

Build a Bridge

Step 4: *Make it OK.*

Is your colleague ready to hear you? If not, it doesn't matter how important your request is or how eloquently you make it. You won't be able to accomplish much of anything if the teammate isn't ready to engage.

> Luis, I'd like to ask a favor of you. May I?

Rarely does someone refuse. Just the act of asking first shows respect. If you don't ask, others may resent you for pushing your uninvited demands on them. When you ask, at least people can decide whether they even want to entertain a request from you at this time.

And what if you are the boss? The answer to that question is the same as when you need to give feedback. Your team members (your subordinates) are not in a position to refuse to hear your requests. It's your job to correct their behavior, delegate tasks, make work assignments, and so on. They may not want to hear your requests, but they are going to hear them anyway, right? In this case, show them respect by ask-

ing about timing. Replace the option of hearing or not hearing your request with the option of *when* they can hear it.

> Luis, I'd like to ask you to do something in a different way.
> Would you like me to do that now, or does after our staff
> meeting work better for you?

If you're Luis's boss, giving him a choice about *when* he
hears your request, instead of *whether* he hears it, recognizes
your right to impose yours or the organization's needs on
him. But it also respects him as an adult, allowing him a say
on timing.

Step 5: *Preface your request with feedback.*

Why are you making this request now? You need to correct
or adjust something that is not working well for you; something needs to be changed. You can be most effective if you
put that request into context first. Preface it with some
BOLD feedback. The feedback sets the stage for why you
are making your request. (See Chapter 5 for information on
how to deliver feedback effectively.)

In this example, see how the feedback delivered to Luis
helps him understand the reasons for the request.

> Luis, when we have our one-on-one meetings, you often
> look at your watch, gaze out the window, or check your
> email while I'm talking. Last week you even opened an email
> and told me to continue talking while you read it. Already
> today, I've noticed you look at your watch twice.
>
> When you do this, it makes me feel like I don't have
> your full attention and flusters me a bit. And even if I do have

your attention, it still makes me feel like my information is less important than what you're doing. That doesn't give me much motivation to really push myself the way you want me to for this project.

Luis is doing things that are getting in the way for me during our update meetings. Just pointing out the undesirable behaviors (and their impact) implies a request. Obviously, I wouldn't bring up the behaviors if I didn't want a change. You'll see that following this feedback with a well-articulated request clarifies exactly what I need from Luis.

It may be tempting to lead your request with positive feedback first—to soften the blow. This tactic can work as long as your transition between the positive feedback and the request is not a *but*. (As we know, *but* means "please disregard everything I've just said, because I'm about to tell you what I really think.") A better word to connect the positive feedback and the request is *and*. It says that both parts of your communication are equally valid and important.

Read each of these examples aloud to hear the effect that just one word can make, and you'll easily understand which sounds better.

> You're doing a great job of documenting all our project changes, Luis. The reports you generate are always current and accurate. That's important when we have to respond to a client inquiry. I really appreciate your staying on top of it so well, *but* I think our update meetings could be more effective if you . . .

> You're doing a great job of documenting all our project changes, Luis. The reports you generate are always current and accurate. That's important when we have to respond to

a client inquiry. I really appreciate your staying on top of it so well, *and* I think our update meetings could be more effective if you . . .

The *and* makes the preceding feedback connected to—and just as important as—the request that follows.

Note that synonyms of *but*—*however, yet, although, nevertheless, though*—have the same effect as *but*. Use *and* instead. As a replacement for *but, and* is always grammatically correct.

Step 6: *Start with deliberate words of assertion.*

How assertive do you come across? Your request can seem soft, forceful, or something in between. Your choice depends on many factors: how strongly you feel about the request, the relationship you have with your teammate, your natural communication style, your position or level of authority, and so on.

Soft requests are made with questions and fairly tentative words. *Stronger* requests use "I" statements and words that are more pointed. The *strongest* requests use "you" statements with demanding words.

These phrases become more assertive as you go down the list:

Luis, would you think about . . . ?
Luis, may I ask you to . . . ?
Luis, would you please . . . ?
Luis, I was hoping that maybe you would. . . .
Luis, I would appreciate it if you would. . . .
Luis, I would like you to. . . .
Luis, I want you to. . . .

Luis, I need you to. . . .
Luis, you're going to want to. . . .
Luis, you need to. . . .
Luis, you have to. . . .
Luis, you must. . . .

The words you choose should match the situation and your goal in making the request. The key is to choose the words deliberately and in advance. Don't settle for whatever comes out of your mouth in the moment. It may be stronger or weaker than what you want or need.

Speak Your Truth

Step 7: *Be specific about what you want.*

What do you want from your teammate? Spell out exactly the behavior you are asking for. Be specific so that there is no misunderstanding about your request. Don't generalize or label the behavior you want because that leaves too much room for interpretation (or rather, misinterpretation).

In the following examples, which is less apt to be misunderstood by Luis?

Luis, I want you to be more respectful of me when we meet and pay better attention.

Luis, I would like you to look me in the eyes when we meet, and not look everywhere else. Maybe even ask me some questions about what I'm reporting on. And please don't look at your watch so much or check email.

The second example leaves no room for misunderstandings. Luis can then be held accountable for making this change—or not—because the request is specific.

Step 8: *Make the request relevant.*

Why do you want this change? What impact will it have on you, your clients, other teammates, sales, internal processes, timelines, projects, and in general? If you can't point to how the change affects the organization, you probably shouldn't be requesting it. Showing the impact helps to avoid arguments about the validity of your request.

Which of these two comments is more likely to convince Luis of the need to change his behavior?

> Luis, I would like you to look me in the eyes when we meet, and not look everywhere else. Maybe even ask me some questions about what I'm reporting on. And please don't look at your watch so much or check email.

> Luis, I would like you to look me in the eyes when we meet, and not look everywhere else. Maybe even ask me some questions about what I'm reporting on. And please don't look at your watch so much or check email. If you do these things, it helps me stay focused and our conversations actually go faster—which I know you'll appreciate. I'll also feel like you value my contribution, and that helps me stay motivated about our project.

Don't feel you have to add emphasis or drama to increase the impact. And certainly don't just make up reasons. Be sure that the claimed impact is actually related to what you are requesting—that there is a true cause-and-effect relationship.

If not, your teammate easily sees through the fabrication, and you lose credibility—on this and future requests.

Compare the last example with the following one. Of the two, which is more believable to Luis and helps him change his behavior in your next meeting?

> Luis, I would like you to look me in the eyes when we meet, and not look everywhere else. Maybe even ask me some questions about what I'm reporting on. And please don't look at your watch so much or check email. If you do these things, we'll be so much more productive that we can probably cut our meeting times in half!

Ideally, you can point out not only how you (or others) will benefit from the change, but also the positive impact on the teammate. This may take some effort to figure out. But if you can think of something, your request is all the more appealing.

Consider the following examples. Which request would be more compelling for Luis?

> Luis, I would like you to look me in the eyes when we meet, and not look everywhere else. Maybe even ask me some questions about what I'm reporting on. And please don't look at your watch so much or check email. If you do these things, it will help me stay focused and I won't get so flustered. And being flustered embarrasses me. I'll also feel like you value my contribution, and that's really important to me. I need to know I make a difference here.

> Luis, I would like you to look me in the eyes when we meet, and not look everywhere else. Maybe even ask me some questions about what I'm reporting on. And please don't

look at your watch so much or check email. If you do these things, it will help me stay focused and our conversations will actually go faster. I'll also feel like you value my contribution, and that will motivate me to work even harder for the team.

The first example is all about me. The second example shows benefit for both of us.

Invite Dialogue

Step 9: *Make it a discussion.*

What kind of reaction might you get from your teammate? Anger? Blaming? Hurt? Confusion? Silence? Defensiveness? Deflecting? Avoidance? An emotional outburst? After you make your request, your teammate may respond either to the preliminary feedback or to the request itself. The better you know your colleague (and the more often you interact like this), the better you are able to predict the response and prepare for it.

You can minimize negative or extreme responses by following the eight steps just discussed. And assuming innocence goes a long way toward diffusing potentially negative situations.

In the event of an immediate emotional reaction, your teammate needs to work through it before being ready to accept your gift of feedback, much less consider changing anything. Everything you have done is wasted if you don't help your teammate past this point or at least allow time for processing feelings. After an emotional reaction, your colleague may want to clarify what he or she sees as a misunderstanding on your part or seek advice on how to proceed. Be prepared for either.

If you don't get much of a reaction, ask for one. Inviting a response may be frightening, but it's essential on a BOLD team. Letting the issue go after you've put out a request is a step back toward NICE. Don't let that happen. Prepare for this part of the discussion by anticipating the reaction so that you are ready to deal with it. Play it out in your mind. Imagine your teammate arguing with you, or blaming you, or doing whatever you expect. Consider different ways to help the team member through a negative reaction and focus on your helpful message.

First and foremost, though, listen without getting defensive. Assume innocence in *their* reaction. Listen to understand. Then acknowledge the feelings, the response, and even the resistance.

Step 10: *Be prepared with a fallback position.*

What if the team member is not willing to agree to your request? Not everyone is going to immediately oblige you. Pride is the most common reason, but other factors play heavily. Regardless of the reason for not accommodating you, you're best off entering the conversation with a backup position. What will you do if your teammate says no?

Reflect on several options before deciding on your backup plan. Initially, you may think that you can do nothing more or that the only alternative is to escalate the situation to a higher authority. Dig deeper and you'll find options.

In this example, you'll see how many options I have if Luis says no:

1. I give up and just tolerate his behavior.
2. I talk to our boss about it.
3. I suggest we hold our meetings in my office instead of his (at least there, he can't check his email).
4. I bring an agenda with an ending time to our meetings and ensure we cover everything in that amount of time.
5. When I'm meeting with him, I check my watch, too, discreetly. Maybe I really *am* taking too long to convey my message. If so, I'll need to adjust how I communicate with him.
6. I become more selective about what I bring to him and use email to share other information. He focuses more on email anyway.
7. I remind myself that his behaviors are not aimed at me personally. Everyone else on the project team complains of the same thing.

Step 11: *Make the discussion a start, not an end.*

What are the next steps for both of you? Even if the teammate agrees to your request, it may not be resolved so simply. The colleague may:

◻ Be unclear about exactly how to change.
◻ Have a counter-request of you that makes it easier to comply with your request.

◻ Need your feedback in order to adjust the behavior.

Be prepared to support your teammate after this discussion is over. FIERCE team members drop the bomb and let their teammates pick up the pieces. If NICE team members even make a request, they back away from it almost as soon as it escapes their lips. BOLD team members, however, make a request and then stick around to facilitate the resolution. Offer your support. Then offer a word of genuine encouragement or confidence.

Making a request is simply speaking out on your own behalf. Respect yourself enough to speak up. Respect your teammates enough to do it appropriately. And trust that your teammates respect you enough to listen and respond.

Use the worksheet in Appendix 5 to outline how to make a request of a teammate.

Summary

◻ Making requests is your way of asserting your needs without being demanding, selfish, or overbearing.

◻ The 11 steps of BOLD requests coincide with the four BOLD principles:

• Step 1: Approach others with respect. *(Assume innocence.)*
  Why should your teammate change anything?

- Step 2: Choose a good time.
  When will you make your request?
- Step 3: Choose a comfortable environment.
  Where will you make your request?
- Step 4: Make it OK. *(Build a bridge.)*
  Is the teammate ready to hear you?
- Step 5: Preface your request with feedback.
  Why are you making this request now?
- Step 6: Start with deliberate words of assertion.
  How assertive will you come across?
- Step 7: Be specific about what you want. *(Speak your truth.)*
  What do you really want from your teammate?
- Step 8: Make the request relevant.
  Why do you want this change?
- Step 9: Make it a discussion. *(Invite dialogue.)*
  What kind of reaction might you get from your teammate?
- Step 10: Be prepared with a fallback position.
  What if the colleague is not willing to agree to your request?
- Step 11: Make the discussion a start, not an end.
  What are the next steps for the both of you?

◆ ◆ ◆

Who timidly requests invites refusal.

LATIN PROVERB

7

BOLD
Disagreements

Behold the turtle. He makes progress only
when he sticks his neck out.

James Bryant Conant

Disagreeing is *not* a matter of being right or making your
teammate wrong. It's *not* about quarreling, bickering, or feu-
ding. And it certainly is *not* about winning or losing. That's
all FIERCE. Disagreeing also doesn't happen just in your
head or later—behind people's backs—so as not to offend or
cause conflict. That's NICE.

Disagreeing with a teammate is merely the act of sharing
an alternate viewpoint or perspective. It's about expressing
your opinion without discounting your teammate's. *Healthy
disagreements* occur when team members highlight differences

in a way that allows everyone to reflect on and consider new alternatives or ones that aren't getting full consideration.

Disagreements are critical to BOLD teams. The greatest value of a team is its diversity of thinking, approach, and style. Most team participants say they want to leverage that diversity, but just voicing differences becomes challenging for them. BOLD teams recognize and respect the outcome of healthy debate. They encourage each other to openly challenge and disagree with each other. They know the difference between disagreeing with, challenging, or even attacking an *idea*, and challenging or attacking an *individual*.

BOLD disagreements, like other BOLD interactions, need compassion and courage. Without compassion, disagreements quickly disintegrate into ego contests, arguments, or worse. Without courage, disagreements rarely even happen. And when they do, they are tentative, so they are not taken seriously. If there are real differences, they are almost immediately minimized or dismissed altogether.

When you disagree openly and respectfully, misunderstandings are quickly resolved. *Most conflict in a group is due to misinformation. Disagreeing is the way to alert the group that more information needs to be shared.* If the additional information doesn't solve the conflict, what you're likely facing is a difference in values or goals. If that's the case, communicating to understand the differences is critical to attaining a consensus on how to proceed.

Here's how to apply the four BOLD principles of teamwork (Chapter 4) as a way to disagree with your teammates appropriately.

Assume Innocence

Step 1: *Begin with a worthy purpose.*

Why are you disagreeing? Ideally, the purpose is to improve your team's work or the decision being made. You want to contribute another perspective that you believe should be explored, considered, or even agreed to before the team proceeds. If this is your intent, that's how you will come across, and you'll be perceived as helpful. So check your intention before speaking up.

You won't help yourself or your teammate if your true desire is to show someone up, to get your way, to be argumentative, to get revenge, to make yourself look smart, or to make someone else look bad. Those motives come across (no matter what polite words you use) and are destructive to the team's process and to your credibility.

Be sure your primary goal is to help the team or a teammate. If your goal is not to help, improve, or strengthen, then figure out what's going on for you, and deal with it in a different, more appropriate way.

Part of assuming innocence means that you find the truth in your teammate's position. Assume that what this person is saying has some inherent value. Find the worthwhile nugget before you proceed, or you'll come across as arrogant, judgmental, or closed-minded.

Step 2: *Choose a good time.*

When will you raise your disagreement? NICE team members wait—and wait so long that the topic changes. Decisions are already made. Going back to the point they wanted to make before feels awkward now, so they hold back. They justify never making the point so as not to disrupt the flow of the current conversation.

FIERCE team members do just the opposite: They interrupt. What they have to say is so important (in their minds) that it can't wait for a teammate to finish a sentence. They break in abruptly and take over the conversation.

BOLD disagreement means that you wait until whoever is talking finishes sharing his or her idea. Understand your teammate's point thoroughly before you jump in with a different perspective. That's almost impossible if you chime in before a person is done speaking.

How do you break in when the discussion is swift? Start with nonverbal cues: lean forward, raise your hand, nod, or make eye contact with an expectant look on your face. If that doesn't work, join the discussion verbally: "Uh-huh, yes. I see. . . . Sure you do. . . . Indeed." Note that all of these are positive, agreeing words (more about this in Step 4); you are not disagreeing yet. You merely join the conversation where it is now, before you present a contrary position.

As a last resort, interrupt. Do this only after you've tried to enter the discussion and found it impossible. Find the closest thing to a pause in the conversation. Excuse yourself. Use the name of the person you are interrupting. State that you'd like to share something before the conversation goes much further, and then encourage your teammate to finish.

See how this can sound:

> Excuse me, Mei. Sorry to interrupt. I'm having trouble keeping up here, and I have something I want to share as well.

When you're finished, may I add something, too? Thanks. Please continue.

Excuse me, Mei and Karen. Wow, you guys are going back and forth so fast, I feel like I'm watching a ping-pong match! I'd like to join in with a point, too. When you're finished, Karen, do you two mind if I jump in? Thanks. Now, Karen, you were saying?

If you wait too long—or if the discussion gets away from you somehow—don't be afraid to go back. What you have to say is important. Trust yourself. Speaking up late is better than keeping quiet. Your perspective will help the team. You'll either change or confirm something. In either case, your voice should be heard.

When the discussion seem like it's about to move on, announce that you want to go back a bit because you have something to share:

Excuse me, everyone. I have a point I wanted to make a while ago when we were discussing the system upgrade. I realized something then that I think we should consider. I know this means backtracking a bit, but I believe it's important. Would you mind if I share that with you now?

In some sensitive situations, waiting until *after* the meeting to disagree may be appropriate. This situation is rare, so be careful. NICE teams often go this route to avoid conflict, when everyone would really benefit from the disagreement being handled in a team setting. Also, discussing disagreement away from the team may be perceived as going behind backs or even sabotaging the team's work. Generally, be courageous and speak up in the moment. If you do disagree off-line, check with your teammate to see how you both can bring the disagreement or the result of it back to the team (see Step 9).

Build a Bridge

Step 3: *First, listen for full understanding.*

What exactly do you disagree with? Note that the word is *what*, not *who*. Be sure you understand your teammate's position before you say anything. If you don't comprehend it, you can't disagree. You can argue or bicker, but you can't legitimately disagree if you don't know what you're disagreeing with.

> Paraphrasing Stephen R. Covey: seek first to understand, and then to be understood.

Pay attention so that you understand the background as well as the immediate topic or issue. Make sure you comprehend the context. Stay in the moment when you listen. Focus on what is being said, not on what you will say next. Listen for points on which you can *agree*, not just disagree.

As you transition from listening to speaking, begin with questions. You can ask questions to either verify or to clarify.

To *verify* (or confirm) that you understand your teammate, simply paraphrase or summarize what you heard. Then ask if you got the gist of it.

> Mei, are you saying we should send an email to everyone about schedule changes when they happen?

It sounds like you're saying that we should send an email out to everyone for every schedule change, is that right?

The other way is to *clarify* your teammate's position. Check your assumptions. You may have heard what they said, but if you took their words and drew conclusions, now is the time to find out if you're correct.

So Mei, are you saying that every schedule change should be communicated with everyone, regardless of how minor the change is?

Mei, it sounds like you're suggesting emails go out to everyone no matter how big or small the schedule change is—even if it's so small that it doesn't affect anyone but us. Is that correct?

Notice the lack of judgment. The assumption about sending emails out to everyone for each schedule change is being checked. The questions are neutral and come from a desire to understand, not to criticize or belittle.

When you clarify, watch that your tone doesn't sound condescending or critical. Honestly and innocently seek to understand before moving forward. The more you understand, the more you can appreciate the other person's perspective. The more you appreciate other people's perspective, the more effective you can be in getting others to understand and appreciate yours.

Listen first. Verify that you understand. Check and clarify your assumptions. Lead off with courtesy and respect. Others will reciprocate.

Understand first—*always*.

Step 4: *Make it OK to disagree.*

Is your teammate ready to hear you? If not, it doesn't matter how important your point is or how eloquently you make it. You won't be able to affect anything if the other person isn't ready to engage.

> Mei, I'd like to share a different perspective about how we may communicate the schedule changes. Would that be OK with you?

As long as you have sincerity in your voice, have timed this right, and truly understand your teammate's perspective, he or she will welcome your input.

Asking permission is important. Asking shows respect. When you ask first and your teammate agrees, you have the floor. But, more importantly, your teammate gave you the floor. Unlike on FIERCE teams, you cannot be accused of being pushy, aggressive, or overbearing because you asked first.

Step 5: *Bridge to your point.*

Where do you agree? That's right: *agree*. Knowing this helps you build a bridge from where you agree to where you disagree. No matter how far apart you feel from someone else's opinion, you can agree on something. Maybe you agree on the goal, but not on how to get there. Perhaps you agree with most of their approach, but not all. Or maybe you agree on just one, single aspect of the subject under discussion, and that's it. Whatever the case, start with the agreement.

Leading off with common ground does three things:

○ *It helps your teammates feel less defensive.* They see that you are not dismissing things out of hand. They see that you have been paying attention and that you understand their position well enough to ferret out what you agree with and what you don't.

○ *It puts things into perspective.* Highlighting the area of agreement *contains* the disagreement. Not everything is up for debate: just this one part or aspect. If you show how close you both are already, your teammate can feel more confident about resolution. The gap doesn't seem so great.

○ *It clarifies one last time that you truly understand their position.* Now you can build off of your agreement.

Consider the following examples. See how the first one actually promotes defensiveness and aggravates disagreement:

But Mei, you fail to see how our staff will react to a broadcast email! This is not going to work for what we want to accomplish. We need to find a better way!

Well Mei, clearly we are together on wanting to communicate the schedule changes in a way that ensures everyone hears the same message at the same time. And I agree that we need to be careful about the words we choose, too. You're right: An email would accomplish those things for us. My concern is about the reaction the rest of the people in the organization will have when. . . .

The second example starts with agreement, helping Mei to see exactly the point of disagreement. It's not as all-encompassing as the generalization of the first example suggests. It leads Mei from agreement to a single point of disagreement, so that she can focus on the one point without being defensive about other areas.

As mentioned already, don't move from agreement to disagreement with the word *but*. *But* means that whatever came before it is less important than what comes after. You want your opening comment of agreement to be seen as just as important as your disagreement or challenge. Use *and*. It bridges your agreement to your disagreement and keeps both parts equally important. Also avoid *but* look-alikes: *however, though, yet,* and *although*.

If you were Mei, which of these examples would feel better to you?

Well Mei, clearly we are together on wanting to communicate the schedule changes in a way that ensures everyone hears the same message at the same time. And I agree that we need to be careful about the words we choose, too. You're right: An email would accomplish those things for us. But I am concerned about the reaction the rest of the people in the organization will have when . . .

Well Mei, clearly we are together on wanting to communicate the schedule changes in a way that ensures everyone hears the same message at the same time. And I agree that we need to be careful about the words we choose, too. You're right: An email would accomplish those things for us. And I am concerned about the reaction the people in the rest of the organization will have when. . . .

Of course, not using *but* or *and* can work just fine. However, if you need a connecting word, use *and*. It bridges agreement to disagreement.

Speak Your Truth

Step 6: *Make your point.*

Where do you disagree? Yes, finally, you get to *say* where you disagree! State specifically how you disagree. NICE team members are tempted to soften their point by using one of these tactics:

- Using tentative language, words like *maybe, perhaps, kind of, sort of*
- Going off on a tangent, leaving your point to head for a safer topic
- Beating around the bush, talking *around* the point, but never saying it directly
- Speaking for, or through, others, refusing to own up to a different opinion

BOLD team members disagree using specifics. They succinctly call out differences of opinion.

Which of the following examples best speaks to the point of disagreement?

I'm concerned about the reaction the rest of the people in the organization will have when they get the emails. I don't know . . . it's just kind of weird. I just think, well, maybe it may not go over very well. But then maybe it will . . . I'm just not sure, I guess. [This language is tentative.]

I'm concerned about the reaction the people in the rest of the organization will have when they get the emails. I mean, we all get so many emails. Half the time I get back to my desk and I get a notice that my inbox is full and emails are being rejected. We just get so many emails already. [This is a tangent.]

I'm concerned about the reaction the people in the rest of the organization will have when they get those emails. It just may be a bit much, is all I'm saying. It just seems like there's got to be a better way that won't be as prominent. So I'm not sure if I'm onboard with the email plan. I don't know if it will really work for us. [Now you're beating around the bush.]

I'm concerned about the reaction the people in the rest of the organization will have when they get those emails. I just think . . . well, I don't know. I think we should be careful here. What do you think, Darryl? Pat? [You're speaking for, or through, others.]

I'm concerned about the reaction the people in the rest of the organization will have when they get those emails. I'm concerned that emails going out every time we have to change the schedule in any way may send the wrong signal: that we can't manage to a time line. And that may cause them to lose confidence in our team. [This is the real disagreement.]

The last example is the only one that pinpoints the objection. With that information, the team is ready to have a meaningful and productive discussion about how to perceive the emails.

When you state your point, be sure to go after the idea, not the person. This helps you and your teammates keep personalities out of the discussion. Keep defensiveness down and the focus on resolution up.

In these examples, which one would make Mei want to defend herself, and which would keep her engaged in problem solving?

I'm concerned about the reaction the people in the rest of the organization will have when they get the emails. I don't think you've thought through your proposal very well, Mei. Can't you see that all the emails will make us lose credibility with them? Or maybe you want them to think we don't know what we're doing. You can't broadcast changes to them all the time!

I'm concerned about the reaction the people in the rest of the organization will have when they get the emails, Mei. I'm concerned that emails going out every time we have to change the schedule in any way may send the wrong signal: that we can't manage to a time line. And that may cause them to lose confidence in our team.

Focus on the issue, problem, or result of the disagreement. Steer clear of personalities, inferences, and judgments that may be affecting the disagreement.

Step 7: *Support your point.*

How is your point relevant? You wouldn't disagree just for the sake of disagreeing. Obviously, you have a reason. Now's the time to share it. Show how your different viewpoint has merit. And don't forget to connect it to some point of agreement.

In this example, the disagreement is strengthened by sharing the logic behind it and by tying it to a common goal for the team:

> I'm concerned that sending emails every time we have to change the schedule in any way may send the wrong signal: that we can't manage to a time line. And that message may cause others to lose confidence in our team. Mei, I think another thing we can all agree on is that we want the rest of the organization to trust that we know what we're doing, right? I'm not sure frequent emails would help us do that.

Mei has been invited to agree on this new point. If she agrees, she must then decide whether the new agreement supports her original position. Meanwhile, her teammate's opposition is supported.

At this point, an alternative may be proposed—or not. See how either option works:

> Mei, I think another thing we can all agree on is that we want the people in the rest of the organization to trust that we know what we're doing, right? I'm not sure frequent emails would help us do that. What if we posted schedule changes on the shared drive? Those who need to know—or want to know—will know where to look. Everyone else

won't be bothered with extra emails, and we won't be calling out the changes so often.

Mei, I think another thing we can all agree on is that we want the people in the rest of the organization to trust that we know what we're doing, right? I don't think that frequent emails will help us do that. I'm not sure what the answer is. I just feel it's important that we consider our reputation, too.

Some organizations have a policy that team members may only disagree if they have a solution as well. "No problems without solutions" is the motto. This kind of policy not only limits whining and negativism, but also encourages individual problem solving. These are good things.

And they come at a cost to the team. Problems or disagreements are identified only by those who have solutions. That means some may sit on critical concerns only because they don't have a solution to offer. Robust problem solving is therefore rare.

Remember: Each team member has one or more strengths. One member may be excellent at finding a weakness in an argument or position; this person may not be so good at figuring out how to solve the weakness. If silenced, that contributor's value to the team is greatly diminished. The team loses. An insight goes unspoken. Another team member may not have the insight to spot the weakness but, if it were highlighted, could find a solution. This person's value to the team is also minimized. Either way, a great solution is never found.

BOLD team members disagree even if they don't have a solution in mind because disagreement is not about faultfinding, but about identifying differences and resolving them. By following the four BOLD principles, they can disagree respectfully, without coming across as whiny or overly negative. Once they share their truth (a disagreement), the whole team has valuable information it can use to solve a problem together. So one team member may identify a problem and another may find the solution. Together, they make the team more successful.

Invite Dialogue

Step 8: *Ask for a reaction.*

How will team members react? If the colleague doesn't respond, ask for a response. If the teammate immediately agrees with you, beware, because they may just be being NICE. Ask the person to elaborate. Without provoking defensiveness, probe to find out if the teammate truly agrees. Open the discussion up to others. Do they also agree?

More often, your teammate does not agree—at least not right away. The NICE team member backs off at this point. The FIERCE team member says the same thing more assertively. BOLD team members, however, step back and assume innocence once again. Ask more questions and listen.

Step 9: *Continue to use the four principles of BOLD.*

How can you and your teammate come to an understanding? Invite the other person to elaborate on the area of disagreement. Repeat the use of the BOLD principles as necessary—

and assume innocence. Ask more questions. Be curious. Seek to understand better. Listen to find common ground again. Build more bridges. Speak your truth more clearly. Finally, if they haven't done so already, invite other team members to join the discussion.

Summary

◻ Disagreeing with someone is simply sharing a different perspective, viewpoint, or opinion.

◻ The four BOLD principles guide the nine steps for BOLD disagreements:

- Step 1: Begin with a worthy purpose. (*Assume innocence.*)
  Why are you disagreeing?

- Step 2: Choose a good time.
  When will you raise your disagreement?

- Step 3: Listen for full understanding first. (*Build a bridge.*)
  What exactly are you disagreeing with?

- Step 4: Make it OK to disagree.
  Is your teammate ready to hear you?

- Step 5: Bridge to your point.
  Where do you agree?

- Step 6: Make your point. (*Speak your truth.*)
  Where do you disagree?

- Step 7: Support your point.
  How is your point relevant?

- Step 8: Ask for a reaction. (*Invite dialogue.*)
  How will they react?
- Step 9: Continue to use the principles of BOLD.
  How can you all come to an understanding?

◆ ◆ ◆

Honest differences are often a healthy sign of progress.

Mahatma Gandhi

8

Become BOLD

Every time I speak my truth, I am looked upon
as being "courageous" and, really, what does
that say about our society? Why isn't that the
norm?

MELISSA ETHERIDGE

You've read seven chapters, all packed with information
about BOLD teams. You're excited about the possibilities.
You can picture your team in its ideal state: BOLD. Now
you're wondering how to pull it all together—especially if
you are the team leader because you're in the best position
to initiate change in your team.

Here are six basic steps to help you start applying what
you've learned. Some exercises you can do as a team to practice BOLD principles in a safe, controlled environment, and
some you may do on your own. Don't feel bound by these

suggestions: If you see a better way to get your team—or yourself—moving toward BOLD, do it!

Caution: Be mindful of your organization's culture, which is a powerful force. If your organization's culture is predominantly NICE, you will quickly be pressured to return to NICE just as you start to venture toward BOLD. Remember that you need courage, compassion, and commitment. The journey won't be easy, but it will be worth it.

Step 1: Have everyone on the team read this book.

Before you can have any meaningful dialogue about your current team or about the team you want to become, you need a common frame of reference. Everyone should be striving for the BOLD teamwork ideal. Your team needs to understand that concept before they can consider it, much less embrace it.

In addition, the book introduces and defines a number of unique terms and phrases: *NICE, FIERCE, BOLD, feedback, assume innocence, disagreement*, and others. A shared vocabulary facilitates discussions about your team.

Step 2: Have everyone complete the NICE Team Assessment in Appendix 1.

The results will be used to prompt a discussion about your team's strengths and weaknesses. Compile the results anonymously, and then share them with the team.

Step 3: Talk about your team.

Use the results of the NICE Team Assessment as a starting point in the discussion, which may be challenging if your team is very NICE. Having a frank discussion about the team is contrary to NICE. Focused questions can help you break the ice.

Here are some questions you may use. Don't try to ask all of them. There are too many on purpose. Pick and choose among them rather than following a script or a "correct" list. Some questions are more direct than others. Because NICE teams have difficulty with direct questions, consider this as you plan the discussion. Lead off with the relatively general (i.e., safe) questions to get the conversation moving.

- What do you think about our results? What do you make of these results?
- What surprised you most about our responses?
- What was the least surprising about our responses?
- Which question was the most difficult for you to answer?
- What question should have been asked on the assessment but wasn't?
- How would you summarize these results?
- What pattern do you see here?
- Where are our obvious strengths as a team?
- How NICE are we?
- When or how often are we FIERCE?
- How accurate was the assessment?

◘   Which questions seemed redundant in the assessment?

◘   How does our organization's culture contribute to our responses on the assessment?

◘   What did this assessment miss in looking at our team?

◘   How would our clients, our business partners, our boss, or others respond to the Assessment about our team?

All of these questions are open-ended, meaning that they require more than a one-word answer ("yes" or "no"). They will generate lots of discussion, so stick with them. If you get a limited or single-word response, follow up with a request for more information:

Do you think we are NICE?

Yes.

Please share with us what leads you to that perception.

The follow-up statement promotes more discussion.

After you ask each question, pause. Give all the members a moment to gather their thoughts before they answer; don't assume that no one will participate. The longer you pause, the more likely people are to eventually speak up. After each response, encourage others to participate, even if all they do is agree. "Who else has an opinion? . . . How do others feel? . . . What else?" Let team members know that the goal is to speak up, not to get a "right" or "definitive" answer.

If your team is large (more than eight or nine people), only a few may participate in a whole team discussion. Divide the team into smaller groups, and hand out or ask three to five questions that each group should talk about. When you get back together as a team, have each small group summarize its findings for the rest of the team. Warmed up now, more people are likely to participate as you consider more questions as a whole team.

Step 4: As a group, agree on the desired state for your team.

Do you want to be BOLD? If so, what does BOLD look like? Decide on a vision together. Don't accept the definition of BOLD given here without debate. Use it as a starting point so that your team can define its own ideal state. Create a vision that everyone can clearly see and that incites them to action.

Use some of these questions to stimulate conversation:

- What, specifically, would BOLD look like if we embraced it?
- How would we behave differently with each other if we were BOLD?
- How are we already exhibiting BOLD behavior?
- What would we lose if we became more BOLD?
- What should we *start doing* that will make us more BOLD?
- What should we *start saying* to help us be more BOLD?
- What should we *stop doing* that keeps us from being BOLD?

◻ What will we *stop saying* that keeps us from being BOLD?

◻ What's in it for each of us, personally, to make the effort to be BOLD?

◻ How should we handle it when we slip and revert to NICE? Or to FIERCE?

◻ What are the inherent risks associated with our move toward BOLD?

◻ How will our clients or customers benefit when we are BOLD?

◻ How will the rest of our organization benefit when we are BOLD?

◻ How will I benefit when we are BOLD?

◻ How can we ensure that we'll each strive to be BOLD and not wait for others to go first?

Because these are more questions than you need, select the ones you think will promote the richest team discussion.

The goal is to get the team excited about the future—to get them to engage. They need to buy into the goal so that they will make the effort to change the team's comfortable, established ways. They need to see the payoff for themselves as well as for the team.

Step 5: Practice BOLD regularly and deliberately as a team.

BOLD doesn't just happen because people say, "Let's be BOLD from now on!" The transition takes a sustained effort on everyone's part to initiate and to follow through on changes in behavior.

One of the most effective ways to make BOLD come alive is to call out BOLD behaviors whenever you see them. This is feedback, of course, so follow the tips in Chapter 5. Be sure to be specific and to link the behavior to how it supports the BOLD environment you're trying to develop.

Practice giving BOLD feedback.

Because BOLD feedback is critical for any kind of development, you should begin working on that as a team. Here are some activities for doing this, along with three pieces of advice. First, choose an activity that is right for your team. Second, don't try all the activities at once. Third, play with one for a while before moving on to another.

- *Activity 1*. Commit as a group to eradicate *but* from your team discussions because the word minimizes the information that precedes it. As a gentle reminder, toss a beanbag at people if they use *but*. (The beanbag is feedback!) Make a game by keeping score of who uses *but* the least. Require team members to contribute a quarter to a jar each time they use *but*.

- *Activity 2*. Go around the room and have each team member give someone else one piece of positive feedback, following the steps in Chapter 5. Be sure the feedback is specific and tied to the organization's needs. It's best—at least the first time you do this—not to make assignments: Let people choose whomever they want to recognize (even if some people get more recognition than others).

- *Activity 3*. Pair up. Select someone outside the group to whom you'd like to give some feedback: a prominent politician, a top athlete, or even just your mother- or father-in-law. Have fun with this! Your partner plays the role of that person (primarily just listening), while you practice giving the feedback. Then have your partner give you feedback on how well you handled each of the eight steps in giving feedback. Switch roles and repeat.

- *Activity 4*. Carve out 15–30 minutes at the end of a team meeting to give each other feedback on the meeting itself. Start with feedback that's fairly general in nature (the agenda, the meeting room logistics, how you managed time, etc.) before zeroing in on more pointed feedback to individuals.

- *Activity 5*. Each team member selects someone *outside* the team to give real feedback to. Use the BOLD Feedback Planning Worksheet in Appendix 4. Pair up. Share with your partner your plan to give BOLD feedback. Ask his or her help on improving your plan, and then revise it. Next, do the same thing for your partner. Give a report at the next meeting on how the feedback session went. The next time, do this for someone *inside* the team.

If none of these fits your situation, have your team brainstorm some ideas on how to improve BOLD feedback in the group. What's working? Where do you need to improve? How can you improve together? Don't take on too much, though. Focus on manageable chunks.

Practice making BOLD requests

When you are ready to work on making BOLD requests (Chapter 6), use any of these activities to get started and to keep improving as a team.

◻ *Activity 1.* Pair up. Pick the name of a person outside the group to whom you want to practice making a request: a prominent politician, a well-known celebrity, or the like. Your partner role-plays that person while you practice giving feedback. Work through all 11 steps of making BOLD requests, giving your partner time to respond and yourself a chance to react. Then have your partner give you feedback on the request you just made: How did you handle each of the 11 steps? Switch roles and repeat.

◻ *Activity 2.* Go around the room, asking each team member to share one thing he or she would request of the team in general, following the 11 Steps of BOLD requests. Someone might ask that everyone empty their old food from the refrigerator at the end of each week. Someone might request that people not congregate outside her cubicle to discuss things. Keep the requests general for now. Be sure you make the request relevant by clarifying what's in it for your teammates, too. The next time you do this activity, make the requests more specific.

◻ *Activity 3.* As a team, craft a BOLD request that your team has of another team, department, vendor, client, or other group. In the process of doing this, follow the 11 steps together, using the BOLD Request Planning Sheet in Appendix 5 as a guide.

◘   *Activity 4.* In pairs, have teammates make requests of each other one on one. Give everyone time to prepare in advance, using the BOLD Request Planning Sheet in Appendix 5. Afterward, share BOLD feedback with each other about how the requests were made. How did you feel about the request? How likely are you to change your behavior?

Again, if none of these activities fits your situation, your team can brainstorm ideas on how to improve making BOLD requests in the group. What's working? Where do you need to improve? How can you improve together? Don't try too much, and continue focusing on manageable chunks.

Practice BOLD Disagreeing

Use these activities to practice BOLD disagreements (Chapter 7) as a team.

◘   *Activity 1.* Assign one team member at the beginning of a meeting to be the devil's advocate, whose job is to disagree with everyone on everything. Use your BOLD feedback skills to give your devil's advocate feedback on how well he or she is initiating *healthy debate* within the team. This job can be exhausting, so switch roles after about an hour or at the next meeting.

◘   *Activity 2.* When a potentially contentious point is made in a team meeting, go around the room and ask each team member to weigh in on it. Encourage disagreement or pushback. Promote healthy debate by asking team members to answer this question: "What is your biggest reservation about this issue?" This probe generates more discussion than asking, "Do you have reservations?" The first question assumes there are reservations and invites people to share them.

◻ *Activity 3*. Pair up. Choose a topic that you disagree on (how to train a puppy, euthanasia rights, where the next Olympics should be held, or almost any topic). Someone in each pair begins by asserting a position. The partner then practices disagreeing (assume innocence, build a bridge, etc.). After five minutes, select another topic of disagreement and reverse roles. Afterward, give each other BOLD feedback on how you disagreed.

◻ *Activity 4*. Give ongoing feedback as a disagreement unfolds in a team meeting. As soon as someone begins to disagree (watch for them to build that bridge!), hold your thumbs up. Keep your thumbs up as long as the debating team members use BOLD principles. If they miss a step or don't do one very well, turn your thumb sideways as a reminder. Turn your thumb back up when they get back on track or down if they don't. Once the thumbs are down, stop everything. As a team, explore how the debate is deteriorating, and use BOLD principles to get realigned. Then resume the discussion.

Once again, tailor these activities to fit your situation. If these don't fit, brainstorm other activities with your team. Cover areas that are working and those that need to be improved, and do all this in bite-size pieces.

As you become BOLD together, continue to call out great, in-the-moment examples of team members being BOLD in their everyday interactions. This tactic does three things. First, it's good practice in giving BOLD feedback. Second, it highlights for everyone how BOLD looks and sounds in real life. Third, it gives the team member who's being BOLD positive reinforcement to repeat that great behavior.

Step 6: Frequently assess your progress toward BOLD as a team.

The real key to success in developing a BOLD team is ongoing vigilance. This step *requires* you to be BOLD. Use BOLD feedback to assess your team's progress. Retake the Nice Team Assessment in Appendix 1. Compare the results now with the results from before. Use BOLD requests to suggest behavioral changes and move the team toward BOLD. And handle differences of opinion with BOLD disagreements.

More Ways to Practice BOLD Outside Your Team

Practicing Feedback

You may practice BOLD on your own, away from work. Nonwork settings present lower-risk opportunities, so experiment with them. Use these first few to become familiar with BOLD feedback (Chapter 5):

◻ *Activity 1.* Practice giving feedback to restaurant wait staff. As you dine, pay attention to the service. You have plenty of time to decide what to say. At the end of the meal, give the server your feedback, following the eight steps of BOLD feedback. Practice positive feedback first (it's easier). After you feel confident, try giving some developmental feedback to the server or to the manager. Here's the trick: See if you can just give feedback *without* moving into making a request. (Don't try to *fix* anything.)

◻ *Activity 2.* Give someone feedback via email. While body language and tone of voice are eliminated, with email you have the opportunity to think about what to say. Write it, read it, reread it, and edit it until it says exactly what you want to convey.

◻ *Activity 3.* Give feedback to someone important to you, perhaps a friend or relative. Consider giving your boss BOLD feedback on his or her management style. Whomever you choose, you may want to tell the person in advance that you are working on your feedback skills. Ask for feedback on how you did.

Practicing Requests

If you want to work on making BOLD requests (Chapter 6), try these exercises:

◻ *Activity 1.* Practice making requests of store clerks, restaurant wait staff, hair stylists, and others who provide a service. Recognize what they do (or don't do) that you would like done differently. Think through what you would *like* them to do. Practice using different levels of asserting words (from "would you please" to "I need you to"), and gauge the reactions you get.

◘ *Activity 2.* Make a request by email. Once again, you don't have body language or tone of voice to use, so e-mails allow you to think about what you want to say in great detail. You can write it, read it, reread it, and edit it until it says exactly what you want. Experiment with different levels of asserting words (try "I was hoping that" and then perhaps "you need to") to see how it looks or feels before you send the request. Practice sending a request by email to a friend or family member before doing this with a teammate.

◘ *Activity 3:* Make a request of your boss, who'll be more willing to hear it from you if you preface it by saying that you are practicing BOLD requests. Use the BOLD Request Planning Sheet in Appendix 5 to prepare. Make it easy on both of you the first time: Ask for something that is doable for your boss. Be sure to request BOLD feedback on how you did.

Practicing Disagreement

Finally, try these exercises for practicing BOLD disagreements (Chapter 7):

◘ *Activity 1.* Send a letter to the editor of your local newspaper about an article you disagreed with. You won't be able to invite dialogue, but writing allows you to articulate your point very deliberately. Be sure to bridge from their story to your point, then support the point appropriately. Ask for feedback on your letter from a teammate, even if you end up never sending it.

○ *Activity 2*. Practice saying aloud phrases like, "I disagree. . . . I have a different opinion. . . . I don't agree with you on that. . . . That's not how I see it. . . . I see things differently." Just feel the words of disagreement come out of your mouth. Hear how they sound in your voice.

○ *Activity 3*. Ask a friend or relative to talk with you about a subject you disagree on. Choose something small, but make sure you care about it (otherwise, it's too easy to revert to NICE). Should parents spank their kids? What should everyone do to save the environment? Does the environment need to be saved? Who was the greatest president of our lifetime? The worst? Let them know you are practicing BOLD disagreements so that they are willing to role-play with you and also give you feedback afterward.

○ *Activity 4*. In a private meeting, disagree with your boss. It may be easier if you warn him or her that you are practicing BOLD disagreement and that you want some BOLD feedback after your discussion.

There's No *I* in Team

It's true: There is no *I* in *team*. But there's a *me* in there somewhere! And your *me* needs to take the responsibility to make your team a success. This is true even if you're not the team leader or if you're new to the team or if you're at a lower level than others on the team. Don't wait for them. Be the first—be the courageous one—to take your step toward BOLD.

Then invite your teammates to join you. Experience the joy of being a part of something bigger than you. Experience BOLD.

◆ ◆ ◆

Coming together is a beginning. Keeping together is progress. Working together is success.

Henry Ford

NICE Team Assessment

Take the NICE Team challenge!

For each of the following statements, indicate whether it is always or usually true of your team (score 3), sometimes true of your team (score 2), or rarely or not true of your team (score 1).

1. We give each other much more positive feedback than we give developmental or constructive feedback. (We may even shy away from giving *any* feedback at all, to avoid the negative stuff.)

2. When we give developmental or constructive feedback, it is often vague or whitewashed so as not to be abrasive or offensive.

3. Much truth is spoken offline or behind people's backs, rather than in the team meeting or directly to an individual.

4. We prefer an optimistic atmosphere in team meetings. We discourage the devil's advocates, naysayers, and party poopers from bringing the rest of us down.

5. Silence during discussions and decisions is common, and it is assumed to mean agreement.

6. We say we encourage open, honest dialogue, but in reality our actions tend to shut down most dissent and disagreement.

7. We never say "no" to our customers or internal clients. We feel this helps keep them happy or satisfied.

8. Almost everything we do seems to be a high priority: Everything is important.

9. We have difficulty meeting initial deadlines, and often we find ourselves renegotiating time lines, resources, and/or deliverables.

10. We defer difficult decisions to our leader (and later we can blame him or her if things don't go well).

11. People gain great influence in the group by being the most vocal, the most persistent, or just the last person to speak.

12. Most of the team stays quiet and just goes along—even if they disagree—as long as the decision doesn't seem to have too much of an effect on them personally.

13. We rarely argue or fight or disagree openly. If we do, we resolve it as quickly as possible, usually by sweeping things under the carpet.

14. We create work-arounds to help us avoid issues, people, or situations we'd rather not deal with directly.

15. Members don't often speak their minds in the team, so real debate rarely happens. And when a rare objection or reservation is expressed, we usually just accept it outright rather than challenge or explore it.

16. We aren't tied down to agendas or time lines when we meet. Nor do we confine ourselves with team roles or responsibilities.

17. When someone asks a question, it *must* be answered. It is easy to derail or distract our team just by asking a tangential question.

18. Staying busy feels right, even if we're not productive

or effective. We work long and hard—but not always smart or focused. Decisions are often revisited, and work is frequently redone.

19. We spend little time or energy discussing our team dynamics, preferring to stay on task rather than get tripped up dissecting who's feeling what or why.

20. We often deal with each other in a passive-aggressive way.

21. We don't hold ourselves accountable: That's the boss's job.

Key

1–28   Your team is probably not a NICE team. Check Chapter 2; your team may be FIERCE.

29–44   Your team may be a NICE team. Read on.

45–63   Your team is likely a NICE team. This book is definitely for you!

Team Member Style Assessment

What kind of team member are you? Only you can say for sure, because your style is determined by what *motivates* you, not necessarily how you *behave*. This assessment helps you quickly and easily identify your style.

Read all of the following nine team member descriptions. Each includes a summary of what motivates that type of person, followed by 10 statements that typify this style. Mark *any* that describe you.

No one will match all 10 statements for a particular style, but the more you check as being true of you, the more likely it is that you have that style.

Still not sure? Try this. Select two or three types that match you best. Then look at what motivates each type. Ask yourself, "If I had to choose between satisfying *this* motivating factor or *that* one, which would be more important to me?"

You also can show the lists that best describe you to your friends and family. Undoubtedly, they will have insights into your style or approach.

Peacemaker—motivated by peace, unity, and harmony

- I am tolerant—very accepting and nonjudgmental of others.
- I am supportive and accommodating because harmonious relationships are important to me.
- I'm good at seeing all sides of an issue.
- I tend to use tentative language (*maybe, perhaps*, etc.).
- I've been accused of being stubborn or passive-aggressive.

- I sometimes ramble or go off on tangents when I talk.
- Others say I go with the flow: I'm sweet, calm, and unpretentious.
- Sometimes I have trouble prioritizing important things.
- I don't like making choices: It's easier to say what I *don't* want than what I *do*.
- I value peace and unity very highly.

Champion—motivated by influence, power, and a sense of justice

- I make just as good—if not better—decisions with my gut than through extensive analysis.
- I'm a natural leader: People look to me for leadership.
- I speak forcefully and with confidence.
- I'm direct and honest: What you see is what you get.
- I'm impulsive and tough-minded—I have a bias toward action.
- Others say I'm strong, confident, and courageous, but also forceful and relentless.
- I like to take charge. Sometimes I take over without even realizing it.
- I'm passionate and energetic; I live life with gusto.
- I'm self-reliant, but also protective of others, especially underdogs.
- I love having an impact on the world around me.

Perfectionist—motivated by correctness

- I'm conscientious and self-controlled.

◻ I compare myself with others, and I am harder on myself than I am on them.

◻ I often use words such as *should* and *ought to*.

◻ I like tight accountability, although it may feel like control to others.

◻ I'm organized: I prefer structure and order in my life.

◻ Others say I'm fair-minded, ethical, and principled, but also judging and critical.

◻ I sometimes take things too seriously.

◻ I agonize over making the right choice because I see things as right/wrong, black/white: I have trouble seeing gray.

◻ I love making every detail perfect.

◻ I don't have time to relax, and, if I do, I don't think I even should.

Energizer—motivated by options, variety, and having a good time

◻ I value having different options and seeing possibilities.

◻ I'm a good risk taker, and I'm good at multitasking.

◻ I communicate with humor, stories, extreme words, and even exaggerations.

◻ I'm optimistic, energetic, versatile, and uninhibited.

◻ I love excitement and trying new adventures.

◻ I'm a visionary; I'm good at inspiring others about possibilities and opportunities.

- Others say I'm fun-loving and spirited, but also that I'm not good at follow-through.

- I'm inspirational and enthusiastic.

- I'm at ease in groups and most social settings.

- I love to have fun and be joyful; I avoid pain and unpleasantness.

Guardian—motivated by safety, security, and togetherness

- I'm a good troubleshooter.

- I'm dutiful, dedicated, and reliable.

- I tend to come alive under adversity.

- I prefer predictability and orderliness.

- I constantly question myself about decisions I've made or what may go wrong.

- I tend to be anxious, especially around authority figures.

- Others say I'm warm and friendly, but also skeptical and pessimistic.

- I sometimes mentally classify others into two camps: us and them.

- I'm extremely loyal to, and trusting of, my family and friends.

- I love feeling safe and secure.

Observers—motivated by knowledge and understanding the world

- I'm not very emotional; I'm more cool and cerebral.

- I like to work by myself, with minimal supervision.
- I prefer to stand back and observe life objectively.
- I tend not to be style-conscious.
- I'm good at making emotionally charged or complex decisions objectively.
- I learn best by myself—from books, the Internet, and other sources.
- Others say I'm observant and perceptive, but also secretive and detached.
- I like meetings to be specific and to the point, preferably with an agenda beforehand so that I can mentally prepare.
- I'm motivated more by the problem than by the reward.
- I'm inquisitive and investigative; gathering and analyzing information is important to me.

Individualist—motivated by feelings of uniqueness and understanding of self

- I deeply feel love, beauty, sorrow, and pain.
- I often long for what is missing; the words "if only" come up a lot in my speaking.
- My feelings are hurt if I'm misunderstood or not appreciated for a unique contribution I make.
- I experience dark moods fully, especially melancholy.
- I often long for what others have.
- Others say I'm intuitive and sensitive, but also melodramatic and elite.
- I'm artistic and creative.

- I am unique and different: a real one-of-a kind.

- I establish warm connections with others; I'm comfortable revealing myself.

- I love feeling unique and special, but I also have a need to better understand myself.

Achiever—motivated by productivity and success

- I make decisions that focus on results.

- I don't understand boredom: I always have stuff to do, and I use to-do lists and progress charts to stay on top of it all.

- I'm persuasive and convincing in my communications.

- I tend to value productivity over process, so shortcuts are OK with me.

- I'm a real go-getter; I have no problem remaining motivated and goal oriented.

- Others see me as ambitious and driven, but they also say I wear facades to impress.

- I'm competent and efficient, and I tend to get impatient with those who are not.

- I'm competitive, and I compete to win!

- I am adaptable for almost any situation or circumstance.

- I love being efficient, productive, and successful.

Helper—motivated by giving and caring for others' needs

- I prefer to make decisions in concert with others I trust.

- I learn best when I'm in groups of people (such as seminars), where I can relate with others.
- I like to offer advice, guidance, and suggestions to others, as well as heartfelt compliments.
- I am sensitive to others' needs, but I'm not quite as in touch with my own.
- I'm approachable, warm, and caring.
- I find it difficult to say "no" to the requests of others.
- Others say I'm nurturing, sacrificing, and giving, but also manipulative and proud.
- I am generous and more comfortable giving than receiving.
- I'm a good listener, showing great interest and empathy.
- I tend to align myself with important or powerful people.

BOLD Conversation Assessment

Take the BOLD Principles Challenge!

After a confrontation (offering feedback, making a request, or disagreeing, etc.) with a teammate, ask yourself the following questions. The more "yes" answers you get, the more likely you were using BOLD principles.

1. Was your message important? Did it need to be shared for the success of your teammate, you, or the team?

2. Did you put any assumptions you had about your teammate aside and approach him or her from a position of caring and trust, assuming innocence?

3. Did you approach your teammate and initiate your conversation in a way that encouraged receptiveness to you?

4. Did how you approached your teammate convey that you genuinely understood and respected his or her position or that you wanted to understand and respect it?

5. Did you speak your truth specifically enough that your teammate was clear about what you were talking about?

6. Was your message authentic—without sugarcoating it, whitewashing it, or otherwise minimizing the essence of your truth?

7. Was your message authentic, without being brutal, abrasive, or otherwise unnecessarily harsh in your delivery?

8. Did you tell your teammate how the issue impacts you?

9. Was the impact you shared free of judgments, criticisms, or accusations?

10. Did you invite your teammate to share his or her perspective?

11. Were you genuinely curious about his or her perspective (rather than just following a protocol)?

12. Did you listen to him or her without formulating a response or looking for ammo for your rebuttal?

13. Can you repeat your teammate's position in a fair and objective way now, to prove that you truly heard him or her?

14. Can you accurately articulate where you and your teammate agree, and where you still disagree?

15. Is your relationship with your teammate stronger now than it was before?

BOLD Feedback Planning Sheet

Assume Innocence	1. Make your feedback sincere. Come from a place of caring.
	2. Make your feedback timely. When will you give the feedback?
	3. Choose a comfortable environment. Where will you give the feedback?

Build a Bridge	4. Make it OK. How will you get permission to offer the feedback?

Share Your Truth	5. Make it specific and objective. What happened?	• Avoid vague language and labels. • Balance feedback with *and*, not *but*. • Avoid discussing what should have happened. • Be fair and accurate.
	6. Make it relevant to the organization. Why does this feedback matter?	• Speak for yourself, not for others. • Refrain from adding emphasis or drama.

Invite Dialogue	7. Make this a discussion. What kind of reaction to you expect?
	8. Make this a start, not an end. What are the next steps for both of you?

BOLD Request Planning Sheet

Assume Innocence	1. Approach with respect—why should they change anything?
	2. Choose a good time—when will you make your request?
	3. Choose a comfortable environment—where will you make your request?

Build a Bridge	4. Make it OK—how will you ask if they are ready to hear you?
	5. Preface your request with BOLD feedback (see Appendix 3).
	6. Start with deliberate words of assertion—how assertive will you come across? What words will you use?

Share Your Truth	7. Be specific about what you want—what do you really want or need from your teammate?	• Identify specific behaviors or actions. • Describe the expected result.
	8. Make the request relevant—why do you want this change?	• Point out how your teammate will benefit from this change.

Invite Dialogue	9. Make this a discussion—what kind of reaction to you expect, and how will you respond?
	10. Be prepared with a fall-back position—what if they don't agree with your request?
	11. Make this a start, not an end—what are the next steps for both of you?

Index

absolutes, 118
accountability
  BOLD teams and, 63
  NICE teams and, 9
Achiever(s)
  and BOLD principles, 106
  on BOLD teams, 75–76
  on FIERCE teams, 51–52, 54
  on NICE teams, 24–26
  self-assessment checklist for, 190
agendas, 65
agreement, 150–153
although, 134, 152
always, 118, 119
and
  with BOLD requests, 133, 134
  as bridge-building term, 96–97, 153
asking permission, 150
assertiveness, 134–135
assuming innocence
  and BOLD disagreements, 145–148
  and BOLD feedback, 110–111
  and BOLD principles, 80–81, 91–93
  and BOLD requests, 128–131, 139
  examples of, 91–93
attention, undivided, 102–103
attitude, 117–118

Biggs, Timothy, 4
blame, 103–104
body language, 103
BOLD disagreements, 143–160
  and assuming innocence, 145–148
  and bridge-building, 148–153
  inviting dialogue within, 158
  practice activities for, 170–172, 174–175
  speaking your truth in, 153–158
BOLD feedback, 109–126
  assuming innocence when giving, 110–111
  and BOLD principles, 124–125

  and BOLD teams, 60–61
  bridge-building when giving, 113–115
  emotional reactions and, 138–139
  planning sheet for, 199–200
  practice exercises for, 167–168, 172–173
  prefacing BOLD requests with, 132–134
BOLD principles, 80–82, 85–107
  and balance, 88–91
  confronting others using, 102–104
  and disagreements, 144–154
  examples of, 91–101
  and NICE-BOLD-FIERCE continuum, 85–88
  and NICE/FIERCE norms, 101
  and NICE team players, 105–106
  see also assuming innocence; bridge-building; inviting dialogue; speaking your truth
BOLD requests, 127–142
  and assuming innocence, 128–131
  and bridge-building, 131–135
  and inviting dialogue, 138–141
  planning sheet for, 203–204
  practice activities for, 169–170, 173–174
  and speaking your truth, 135–138
BOLD teams, 59–84
  characteristics of, 59–84, 88–91
  exercises for developing, 161–176
  as goal, xi
  interaction among members of, 66–77
  and NICE-BOLD-FIERCE continuum, 87
  norms of, 77–79
  reasons for success of, 60–66
  requirements for members of, 79–80
boss(es)
  and BOLD disagreement practice, 175
  and BOLD feedback practice, 173
  and BOLD request practice, 174
bridge-building
  and BOLD disagreements, 148–153
  and BOLD feedback, 113–115

bridge-building (*continued*)
  and BOLD principles, 81
  and BOLD requests, 131–135
  examples of, 93–97
but, 96, 97, 133, 134, 152, 167

caring
  and BOLD feedback, 111, 125
  and BOLD teams, 79
Champion(s)
  and BOLD principles, 105
  on BOLD teams, 68–69
  on FIERCE teams, 44–45, 54
  on NICE teams, 14–16
  self-assessment checklist for, 186
Churchill, Winston, on having enemies, 57
clarification
  and BOLD disagreements, 149, 151
  and BOLD feedback, 116–119
compassion
  balancing courage with, 90–91, 110
  and BOLD debate, 63
  and BOLD feedback, 90–91, 110
  and BOLD teams, 88–89
Conant, James Bryant, on disagreements, 143
conflict
  and BOLD debate, 63
  and FIERCE teams, 39–40
  and NICE teams, 9–10
confrontation
  and BOLD principles, 81, 102–104,
    195–196
  and NICE teams, 9–10
constructive feedback, 5
Cosby, Bill, on trying to please everybody, 75
courage
  balancing compassion with, 90–91
  and BOLD teams, 80, 89–91
  and speaking your truth, 98
Covey, Stephen R., on understanding, 94, 148
criticism, feedback vs., 109
culture, 162
curiosity, 100, 101

deadlines, FIERCE teams and, 38, 40
debate, BOLD teams and, 64
decisions
  by BOLD teams, 63
  by FIERCE teams, 40–41
  by NICE teams, 8–11
decisiveness, FIERCE teams and, 38–39
developmental feedback, 5
devil's advocate, 6–7
dialogue, *see* inviting dialogue
direct communication, 103

direction, feedback vs., 109
disagreements, *see* BOLD disagreements

efficiency
  and BOLD teams, 65–66
  and FIERCE teams, 41–42
  and NICE teams, 12
email
  and BOLD feedback practice, 173
  and BOLD request practice, 174
emotional reactions, 138–139
empathy, 104
Energizer(s)
  and BOLD principles, 105
  on BOLD teams, 70–71
  on FIERCE teams, 46–47, 54
  on NICE teams, 18–19
  self-assessment checklist, 187–188
environment, comfortable
  for BOLD feedback, 112–113
  for BOLD requests, 130–131
Etheridge, Melissa, on courage, 161
eye contact, 102–103

failure, FIERCE teams and, 48
faith, 80
fallback position, when preparing BOLD re-
    quests, 139–140
feedback
  BOLD, *see* BOLD feedback
  and BOLD requests, 132–134
  emotional reactions and, 138–139
  and FIERCE teams, 36–37
  and NICE teams, 5–6
  practice exercises for, 167–168, 171
FIERCE teams
  characteristics of, 33–57
  effect of style on members of, 42–53
  and NICE-BOLD-FIERCE continuum,
    86–87
  and NICE teams, 35–42
  norms of, 53–55
flexibility
  and BOLD teams, 64–65
  and NICE teams, 10–11
focus on task, *see* task, focus on
Ford, Henry, on teamwork, 176
forming, 2
four BOLD principles, *see* BOLD principles

Gandhi, Mahatma, on honest differences, 160
generalizations, avoiding, 116–119
Goethe, Johann Wolfgang von, on applying
    knowledge, 73
Griffin, Kathy, on manners, 4
Guardian(s)
  and BOLD principles, 105
  on BOLD teams, 71–72
  on FIERCE teams, 47–49, 54

on NICE teams, 19–21
self-assessment checklist for, 188

healthy debate, 64
healthy disagreements, 143–144, 170
Helper(s)
    and BOLD principles, 106
    on BOLD teams, 76–77
    on FIERCE teams, 52–53, 54
    on NICE teams, 26–29
    self-assessment checklist for, 190–191
hindsight, feedback vs., 109
Holiday, Billie, on individualism, 74
however, 134, 152

Idle, Eric, on hurtful words, 109
imperfections, 69–70
improvement, feedback and, 110, 111
independence, FIERCE teams and, 55
Individualist(s)
    and BOLD principles, 105
    on BOLD teams, 74–75
    on FIERCE teams, 50–51, 54
    on NICE teams, 23–24
    self-assessment checklist for, 189–190
inflexibility, FIERCE teams and, 40–41
information sharing, 144
innocence, assuming, *see* assuming innocence
intent, BOLD feedback and, 111
interpersonal problems
    and FIERCE teams, 41–42
    and NICE teams, 12
interruption, BOLD disagreements and, 146
inviting dialogue
    and BOLD disagreements, 158
    and BOLD feedback, 122–124
    and BOLD principles, 81–82, 100–101
    and BOLD requests, 138–141
    examples of, 100–101

James, William, on conflict and attitude, 107

Kuhn, Maggie, on speaking one's mind, 72

leaders, deferring of decisions to, 8–9
location, *see* environment, comfortable
Lucado, Max, on conflict, 85

making your point, 153–155
Martin, Judith, on not being kind, 31
M★*A*★*S*★*H,* 1
meetings, BOLD teams and, 65
misunderstandings, 144
myths
    about FIERCE teamwork, 35–42
    about NICE teamwork, 5–14

names, using, 102
negative feedback
    and BOLD teams, 113
    and FIERCE teams, 36

never, 118, 119
nevertheless, 134
NICE-BOLD-FIERCE continuum, 85–88
NICE feedback, 5
NICE teams
    assessment exercise for, 179–181
    BOLD principles for changing style of,
        105–106
    characteristics of, 1–31
    and communication, ix–x
    disagreement style of, 153
    and FIERCE teams, 35–42
    followup questions after assessment of,
        163–165
    myths accepted by, 5–14
    and NICE-BOLD-FIERCE continuum,
        85–86
    stalling of development of, 2–4
nonverbal cues, 103, 146
norming
    and FIERCE teams, 35
    and NICE teams, 3, 4
norms
    of BOLD teams, 77–79
    of FIERCE teams, 53–55
    and NICE-BOLD-FIERCE continuum,
        101
"no," saying, 7–8

objectivity, 98
Observer(s)
    and BOLD principles, 105
    on BOLD teams, 73
    on FIERCE teams, 49–50, 54
    on NICE teams, 21–22
    self-assessment checklist for, 188–189
openness, of NICE teams, 10–11
options
    and BOLD feedback, 120
    and BOLD requests, 139–140
organizational culture, 162
overwork, by FIERCE team members, 37–38

passive-aggressive behavior
    and FIERCE teams, 43
    and NICE teams, 12
past tense, for BOLD feedback, 119
Peacemaker(s)
    and BOLD principles, 105
    on BOLD teams, 66–68
    on FIERCE teams, 42–44, 54
    on NICE teams, 13–14
    self-assessment checklist for, 185–186
pecking order, on NICE teams, 8–9
Perfectionist(s)
    and BOLD principles, 105
    on BOLD teams, 69–70
    on FIERCE teams, 45–46, 54
    on NICE teams, 16–17
    self-assessment checklist for, 186–187

performing
  and BOLD teams, 77
  and FIERCE teams, 34
  and NICE teams, 3
permission, asking, 150
planning
  and BOLD teams, 64–65
  and FIERCE teams, 37
  and NICE teams, 6–7
positive feedback
  and BOLD feedback, 113
  and BOLD principles, 124–125
  and BOLD teams, 61
  and FIERCE teams, 36–37
  practice exercises for, 167–168, 173
  setting for delivering, 113
praise, NICE teams and, 5–6
principles, *see* BOLD principles
problems, identifying, 157–158
purpose, in BOLD disagreements, 145

reactions, allowing, 104, 123
relationships
  and BOLD requests, 127
  and FIERCE teams, 35, 39–40
  and NICE teams, 12
relevance
  of BOLD feedback, 121–122
  of BOLD requests, 136–138
re-norming, 4
requests, *see* BOLD requests
resolution
  and BOLD debate, 63
  and BOLD disagreements, 144, 158
  and BOLD principles, 82, 100
  and inviting dialogue, 100
respect
  and BOLD requests, 128–129, 141
  and BOLD team members, 63
  and NICE team members, 8–9
responses, inviting, 123, 139
responsibility to your team, 175–176
restaurants, 173
risk, avoiding, 46–47
roles, unclear, 11

Sapirstein, Milton R., on differing opinions, 73
saying "no," 7–8
saying "yes," *see* "yes," saying
Seuss, Dr., on speaking honestly, 59
Shakespeare, William, on being true to one's self, 84
shared accountability, 63
silos, 11
sincerity, 110–111
soft requests, 134
solutions, disagreements and, 157

speaking your truth
  and BOLD disagreements, 153–158
  and BOLD feedback, 115–121
  and BOLD principles, 81, 97–100
  and BOLD requests, 135–136
  examples of, 97–100
specificity
  for BOLD feedback, 116–119
  and speaking your truth, 98, 135–136
Spencer, Herbert, on boldness, xii
storming
  and BOLD teams, 77
  and FIERCE teams, 34, 35
  and NICE teams, 3, 4
strong requests, 134
success
  and Achievers, 75
  and FIERCE teams, 48
supporting your point, 156–158

task, focus on
  by FIERCE teams, 37
  by NICE teams, 6–7
teams, *see* BOLD teams; FIERCE teams; NICE teams
Thompson, Dorothy, on peace and conflict, 67
though, 134, 152
timing
  of BOLD disagreements, 145–148, 150
  of BOLD feedback, 95–96, 111–112, 114–115
  of BOLD requests, 129–130, 132
tone of voice, 103
trust, 80
truth
  on BOLD teams, 85, 87
  on NICE teams, 85, 86
  speaking your, *see* speaking your truth
Tuckman, Bruce, 2
Twain, Shania, on honesty, 127

understanding, listening for, 148–149
undivided attention, 102–103

vague terms, clarifying, 116–119
venting, 6
verification, 148–149
Voltaire, on honest people, 126

wait staff, 173
Wilde, Oscar, on ideas, 71
winning, resolution vs., 82
work, BOLD teams' attitude towards, 61–62

"yes," saying
  BOLD teams and, 62–63
  NICE teams and, 7–8
yet, 134, 152
your, 97–98

About the Author

Brian Cole Miller is a team builder and facilitator who helps people work together in an open, direct, and honest way. He believes that it's a disservice to individuals and teams to protect them from the truth but that you also don't have to be brutally honest to be effective in relationships. Brian's mission is to show how to achieve effective balance in communications—at work, at home, or in the community—so that teams can get the results they want.

With a master's degree in human resources development and over 25 years of field experience, Brian speaks at conferences around the world. He works with large and small businesses, government entities, and not-for-profits. He teaches at community colleges and universities.

People enjoy working with Brian because of his insight, humor, creativity, and incredible energy. He is available for speaking engagements, meeting/team facilitation, team building, and private consultation.

For additional information and resources on developing BOLD teams, visit www.NiceTeamsFinishLast.com.